IN PARTNERSHIP WITH
IWM

WORLD WAR II

THE DEFINITIVE VISUAL HISTORY

IN WORDS, PHOTOGRAPHS AND RARE ARCHIVE DOCUMENTS

VOLUME I

FROM THE MUNICH CRISIS TO THE BATTLE OF KURSK, 1938–43

RICHARD OVERY

WELBECK

GENERAL MAP KEY TO SPREAD MAPS

Military units

XXXXX
Army Group

XXXX
Army

XXX
Corps

XX
Division

X
Brigade

III
Regiment

II
Battalion

I
Company

Military types

Infantry

Armour

Mechanised

Nationalities

German

Italian

Japanese

United States

British

Soviet

French

Romanian

Finnish

Vichy (named)

Hungarian

other (named)

THIS IS A WELBECK BOOK

Design and map copyright © Welbeck Non-fiction Limited 2020

Text copyright © Richard Overy 2008, 2009

Imperial War Museum photographs and memorabilia
© Imperial War Museum

This edition published in 2020 by Welbeck
An imprint of the Welbeck Publishing Group
20 Mortimer Street
London
W1T 3JW

Originally published in four volumes by Carlton Books in 2008–2009 as *The Second World War Experience: Blitzkrieg 1939–41*; *Axis Ascendant 1941–42*; *Turning of the Tide 1942–43*; *The Struggle for Victory 1944–45*.
This edition contains a selection of material from *Blitzkrieg 1939–41*, *Axis Ascendant 1941–42* and *Turning of the Tide 1942–43*.

Printed in Dubai

A CIP catalogue for this book is available from the British Library

ISBN: 978 0 233 00620 8

Cover photographs
Front: Georgi Zelma/Slava Katamidze Collection/Getty Images
Back: Imperial War Museums, London (H 003233)

28–30 SEPTEMBER 1938

THE MUNICH CRISIS

After Hitler had taken over his Austrian homeland in March 1938, he began to make preparations to seize Czechoslovakia on the pretence that he was helping fellow Germans oppressed by Czech rule in the Sudeten areas of northern Czechoslovakia. On 28 May, following the "Weekend Crisis" of 20/21 May, when the Czech government, fearing an imminent German invasion, ordered the mobilization of its forces, Hitler told his military commanders to plan a short, sharp war against the Czechs for the autumn of 1938. "I am utterly determined," he said, "that Czechoslovakia should disappear from the map."

Hitler thought he could isolate the Czechs and reach a quick military solution before the other powers intervened. The military planning went ahead, reflecting Hitler's anxiety to wage a small, victorious war. In February, he had scrapped the War Ministry and taken over supreme command of the armed forces himself. The fight against the Czechs was a way of making his mark as a military leader, and an opportunity to improve Germany's economic and strategic position in central Europe.

The crisis could not be isolated: as pressure built up on the Czech government to make concessions to the Sudeten German minority, Britain and France both acted to try to find a negotiated political solution. France had treaty obligations to help the Czech state, and the Soviet Union was also committed to intervening, as long as France did so too. In neither state was there much enthusiasm for the prospect of war. Britain, meanwhile, had no treaty obligations, but the Prime Minister, Neville Chamberlain, hoped to use his influence to bring about a negotiated settlement as part of his strategy of "appeasement" of Germany. In August 1938, the British politician Lord Runciman was sent on a League of Nations mission to the Sudetenland and returned arguing that major concessions should be made by the Czech government to the German community.

Hitler stuck to his guns. German leaders attacked the Czechs in the press and on the platform. By the beginning of September, it seemed likely that Hitler would launch the military campaign in the near

13 MARCH 1938
Austria united with Germany in a Greater German Reich.

20–21 MAY 1938
"Weekend Crisis" sees Czech mobilization against a possible German strike.

28 MAY 1938
Hitler orders armed forces to prepare "Case Green" for invasion of Czechoslovakia.

11 JULY 1938
Japanese and Soviet forces spark frontier clash at Changkufeng on Manchurian border.

28 AUGUST 1938
Runciman Mission draws up plans for Sudeten autonomy.

9 NOVEMBER 1938
German pogrom against the Jews on the "Night of Broken Glass".

Czechoslovakia 1938–39

Munich Agreement, October–December 1938

Annexations, 1939

- Czechoslovakia, early 1938
- to Germany
- to Hungary
- to Poland
- Czechoslovakia, Dec. 1938
- to Germany
- Independent
- to Hungary

INTRODUCTION

The Second World War was the largest and costliest war in human history. Its scale was genuinely global, leaving almost no part of the world unaffected. At its end the political geography of the world was transformed and the stage set for the emergence of the modern states system. While it is possible to exaggerate the break represented by victory in 1945, the change between the pre-war world of economic crisis, European imperialism and militant nationalism and the post-war world of economic boom, decolonisation and the ideological confrontation of the Cold War was a fundamental one.

OPPOSITE German soldiers storm part of the Red October plant near the edge of the Volga River in the heart of Stalingrad. Each building was fought for room by room.

It is worth remembering that no-one at the start could be certain what direction the war might take or could anticipate the degree of destruction and violence that it would draw in its wake. A number of different areas of conflict coalesced, like separate fires growing into a single inferno: the European conflict over German efforts to break the restrictions imposed after her defeat in the First World War; the conflicts generated by an expansionist and ambitious Fascist Italy whose leader, Benito Mussolini, dreamed of re-creating the Roman Empire; the war for Asia fought in the east by Imperial Japan, determined to assert the right of non-white peoples to a share of empire; finally, a conflict in Eastern Europe waged by an alliance of anti-Communist states grouped around Hitler's Germany in a crusade against the new Soviet system in 1941.

As the war grew in scope all the major powers were drawn in. It is often asserted that the entry of the United States in December 1941 made victory certain for the Allied powers through sheer economic weight, but the outcome was not pre-ordained. Germany and her allies had large resources and captured yet more. German and Japanese forces fought with high skill. To win the war the Allies needed to improve fighting power, to co-ordinate their activities and to keep their populations – even in times of tribulation – committed to the cause. The idea that the Axis powers, and Germany in particular, lost the war through their own ineptitude distorts the extent to which the Allies had to learn to fight with greater effectiveness and to exploit their own scientific, technical and intelligence resources to the full. It is a measure of the significance they all gave to the war, not simply as the means to their own survival, but as a way to impose one world order or another, that they made the sacrifices they did. There was a powerful sense that this really was a war that would shape the way history would be made.

World War II: The Difinitive Visual History is the story of that conflict from its roots in the 1930s to the final victory of the Allies with the Japanese surrender in August 1945. Following the defeat of the Axis states it proved possible to construct a more stable and enduring world order, though one divided by the Cold War and overshadowed by the threat of nuclear destruction. The two volumes cover the whole period of the war and the many areas of global conflict, in Europe, Asia, the Middle East, Africa and the Atlantic and Pacific Oceans. The first volume begins with the crisis in Europe provoked by the rise of Hitler and his ambitions to turn Germany into a major world power. It charts the early stages of the war in which the Allied powers found themselves faced with one disaster after another – the defeat of Poland, the collapse of Anglo-French resistance in 1940 and the desperate efforts made by Britain and her Empire to avoid defeat in 1940 and 1941. It shows how the war expanded with the entry of Italy on the side of the Axis in June 1940, the conquest of the Balkans by Italy and Germany and then the monumental decision taken by Hitler late in 1940 to attack the Soviet Union in June 1941. This colossal campaign changed the nature of the war to make it truly global. Japan took advantage of the German-Soviet war to attack colonial possessions in south-east Asia and the western Pacific and within months had carved out a vast new empire. By 1942 the Axis seemed unstoppable but during the autumn of 1942, at Stalingrad, at Alamein and on the island of Guadalcanal, the Axis advance was halted and then slowly reversed. The volume ends with the first heavy defeats inflicted on the aggressor states at Stalingrad and on Guadalcanal in January 1943, Tunisia in May 1943, Kursk in July 1943. The war was by no means won but the Allies had learned a great deal from their enemies and Allied fighting power was now equal to the long and arduous task of securing unconditional victory.

RICHARD OVERY, SEPTEMBER 2019

CONTENTS

Neville Chamberlain marches past an SS guard of honour at Oberwiesenfeld airport on his way to the Munich Conference on 29 September 1938, surrounded by National Socialist Party leaders.

future. To avert this, on 15 September Chamberlain took the dramatic step of flying to meet Hitler at his mountain retreat at Berchtesgaden. Chamberlain conceded the need for self-determination, while Hitler promised not to make war on the Czechs, he had no intention of honouring his word. Chamberlain flew again to meet the German leader on 22 September at Bad Godesberg, and this time the atmosphere was quite different, with Hitler insisting that he would occupy the Sudeten areas no later than 1 October. Chamberlain returned home to a cabinet now determined not to concede. France and Britain both prepared for war and on 26 September, Chamberlain sent his personal envoy, Sir Horace Wilson, to see Hitler. On the following day he made it absolutely clear that German violation of Czech sovereignty would mean war.

On 28 September, Hitler, with great reluctance, gave in. Under pressure from his party leaders and aware that German public opinion was strongly against a European war, he accepted Mussolini's suggestion of a summit conference in Munich, to which the Soviet Union was not invited. Hitler was sulky and ill at ease throughout the Munich discussions, which ended

EDVARD BENEŠ
(1884–1948)

The Czech politician at the heart of the Munich crisis was a statesman of wide experience. Beneš had been active in the Czech independence movement during the First World War and was rewarded in 1918 with the post of Foreign Minister in the newly independent Czechoslovak Republic. In 1935, he became the country's president, by which time Czechoslovakia was the only genuinely democratic state left in central and eastern Europe. In 1938, he realized that his country was vulnerable to German pressure and had little confidence that his allies would support him. He went into exile abroad in October 1938 and returned to be president again between 1945 and his death three years later.

ARRIVEE DEPART

KONRAD HENLEIN
(1898–1945)

The Germans who inhabited the so-called "Sudeten" provinces of Czechoslovakia were former German subjects of the Habsburg empire. Many wanted to live in a larger German state and they formed the Sudeten German Party to campaign for autonomy and to agitate for union with Germany. Their leader was the former bank clerk Konrad Henlein. By 1938, the party had 1.3 million members out of a population of only three million. Henlein co-operated secretly with the Hitler government in 1938, refusing the concessions made by the Czech government and increasing tension in the province. He became the first Gauleiter (district leader) of the Sudetenland in 1939, and committed suicide at the end of the war.

on 30 September with an agreement for the cession of the Sudeten areas to Germany and a timetable for German occupation. Unlike Japan in Manchuria and Italy in Abyssinia, Hitler's plan for a short war of conquest was frustrated. Munich is usually seen as a humiliating defeat for the British and French, but in reality it was a defeat for Hitler's plan for war. His frustration was to make it impossible to negotiate away the next crisis in 1939 over the City of Danzig.

ABOVE French premier Edouard Daladier is greeted by enthusiastic crowds on his return to Paris on 30 September 1938. "The blind fools" was his reaction to their welcome.

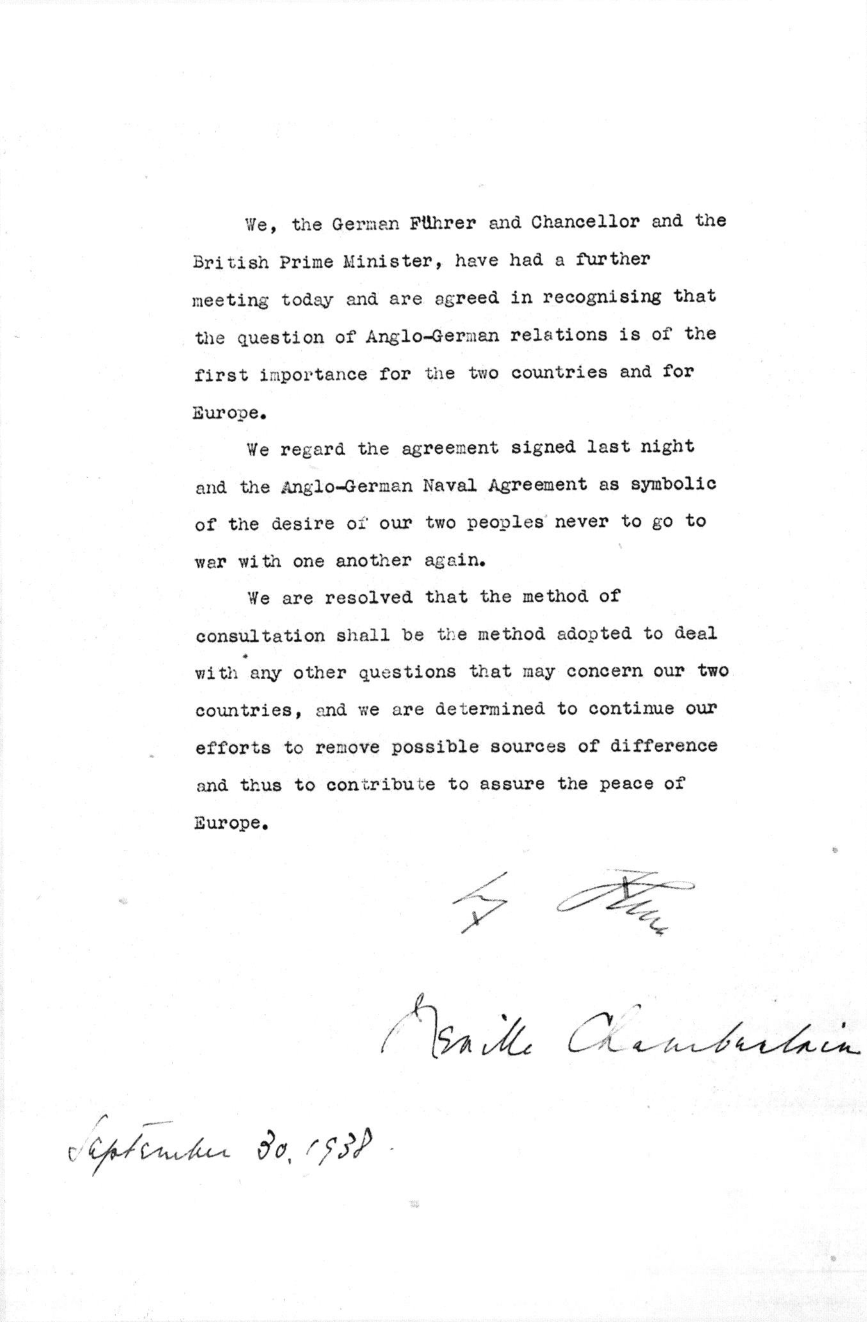

We, the German Führer and Chancellor and the British Prime Minister, have had a further meeting today and are agreed in recognising that the question of Anglo-German relations is of the first importance for the two countries and for Europe.

We regard the agreement signed last night and the Anglo-German Naval Agreement as symbolic of the desire of our two peoples never to go to war with one another again.

We are resolved that the method of consultation shall be the method adopted to deal with any other questions that may concern our two countries, and we are determined to continue our efforts to remove possible sources of difference and thus to contribute to assure the peace of Europe.

[signature]

[signature: Neville Chamberlain]

September 30, 1938.

THE MUNICH AGREEMENT

The Munich Agreement, the Anglo-German declaration of 30 September 1938 signed by Adolf Hitler and Neville Chamberlain.

15 MARCH 1939

THE OCCUPATION AND BREAK-UP OF CZECHOSLOVAKIA

Almost as soon as the ink was dry on the Munich greement, Hitler told his foreign minister, Joachim von Ribbentrop, that he would march on Prague and smash the "Czech remnants" when the opportunity came. The Czech state was put under pressure to reach advantageous trade agreements to help German rearmament, and to concede the right to build a motorway across Czech land. In the Slovak areas, the Germans collaborated with the Slovak separatist movement, putting pressure on the Prague government to grant independence. Bit by bit, the Czech lands were being drawn into the German orbit.

The isolation of Czechoslovakia after Munich also encouraged its other neighbours to join in the search for spoils. On 30 October, Poland demanded the cession of the Teschen region and the Czech government complied; on 2 November, territorial concessions were made to Hungary in southern Slovakia. Germany then demanded that the Prague government turn Czechoslovakia into a virtual German dependency. It was only a matter of time before the remaining Czechoslovak area was broken up. On 12 January 1939, orders were issued to German army units to prepare to occupy the Czech lands, though no final decision had yet been taken. The immediate trigger for the actual invasion was the breakdown in relations between the Czechs and the Slovaks: in March, the Slovak government in Bratislava refused to abandon its claim for independence, thereby

30 OCTOBER 1938
Poland occupies Teschen region of northern Czechoslovakia.

NOVEMBER 1938
Vienna Awards grant territory in Slovakia and Ruthenia to Hungary.

OCTOBER 1939
Czech university students demonstrate on the streets of Prague against German occupation.

BELOW Jewish shops in the Slovak capital of Bratislava destroyed the day before German occupation of the Czech areas of the country, 14 March 1939.

OPPOSITE German troops march into Prague during the occupation on 15 March 1939. Following the takeover the Czech army was disbanded.

TREATMENT OF THE JEWS IN THE CONQUERED LANDS

German occupation of Austria in March 1938 and the Czech lands in March 1939 brought large Jewish communities under German control. Major Jewish businesses and shareholdings were seized to secure Austrian and Czech industry for the German rearmament effort. Thousands of small Jewish businesses were closed down or sold to "Aryan" owners; Jewish professionals were sacked and forced to abandon their possessions if they sought exile abroad. Other countries were reluctant to issue visas since there had already been a steady stream of refugees seeking asylum from National Socialism. Around 130,000 Austrian Jews were able to emigrate before the war, and 35,000 Czech Jews. Those who remained were almost all exterminated.

CZECHS IN THE SECOND WORLD WAR

Many Czechs who fled from German occupation in 1938–39 ended up in France and Britain. When war came, the skilled Czech workers took up jobs in industry or as mechanics in the British armed forces. A number joined the RAF and fought through the Battle of Britain. There were four squadrons or Czech airmen, one bomber and three fighter squadrons. A Czech armoured brigade of 5,000 men was formed and later fought in the north-west campaign. Czech military intelligence officers who came to Britain also played an important role in the British counter-intelligence programme.

Enthusiastic Germans remove the frontier posts separating Germany from Czechoslovakia. The Czech lands became a Reich Protectorate, while Slovakia won its "independence".

Hitler greets leaders of the German community in Prague on 15 March 1939 in Hradcany Castle following German occupation. To his right stand Himmler and the head of the Reich Security Service, Reinhard Heydrich.

provoking the Prague government to declare martial law and send troops into Slovakia. The leader of the Slovak separatists, Jozef Tiso, fled to Vienna and then to Berlin, where Hitler encouraged him to call the Slovak assembly together, which then declared independence on 14 March.

The Czech president, Emil Hácha, took the train to Berlin to seek Hitler's advice, and in the early hours of 15 March, after Hermann Göring had painted a vision for him of German bombers over Prague, he invited Germany to occupy and "protect" Czechoslovakia. At six o'clock in the morning, German forces occupied the Czech provinces of Bohemia and Moravia, while the Hungarian army seized control of some Slovak provinces. The following day, the Czech areas were declared a German protectorate and the former German foreign minister Constantin von Neurath was appointed first "Reich Protector". Major Czech businesses, including the famous Skoda armaments complex, were brought under direct German control, and Czech military supplies helped to equip 15 German infantry divisions and four armoured divisions for the coming

conflict. Slovakia was made an independent pro-German state under Tiso and remained a close ally down to 1944.

The occupation of the rest of Czechoslovakia tore up the short-lived Munich agreement. The British and French governments could do nothing to save Czechoslovakia, which had not actually been invaded but forced to "invite" German occupation, but the decision to incorporate non-German peoples in the new German empire prompted Neville Chamberlain on 17 March to make a powerful speech condemning German action. The Prague occupation had finally convinced him that there was no room for a negotiated settlement and he warned that if any nation tried to dominate Europe, Britain would resist "to the utmost of its power". A few days later, prompted by warnings from the security services of an imminent German occupation of Poland, Chamberlain offered the historic guarantee of Polish sovereignty in the House of Commons on 31 March. The Czech crisis had paved the way for the final countdown to war.

1 SEPTEMBER 1939

GERMANY INVADES POLAND

The German invasion of Poland on 1 September 1939 was the culmination of a plan codenamed "Case White" which had first been drawn up by the German armed forces on Hitler's orders in April. The war against Poland was not a conflict Hitler had initially expected. After Munich, he assumed that the Poles would be drawn into the German sphere of influence. He wanted them to readjust the status of Danzig, a city supervised by the League of Nations to allow Poland access to the sea, to become a German city as it had been before 1919, and to hand back the rich industrial areas of Silesia, which had been given to Poland after a plebiscite in 1919.

The Poles refused any concessions and Hitler, frustrated at not getting his small war in 1938 against the Czechs, decided to punish the Poles by seizing the areas by force. He argued to the doubters in Berlin that Britain and France would protest but would not intervene. After signing the pact with the Soviet Union, Hitler was certain that the risk was much reduced. A pretence at last-minute negotiation in the final days of August was designed to make it seem as if Germany had a legitimate cause for war, though in fact the SS – the elite National Socialist security force – planned to stage a frontier incident to make it look as if the Poles were the aggressors. An attack by Germans wearing Polish uniforms on the frontier

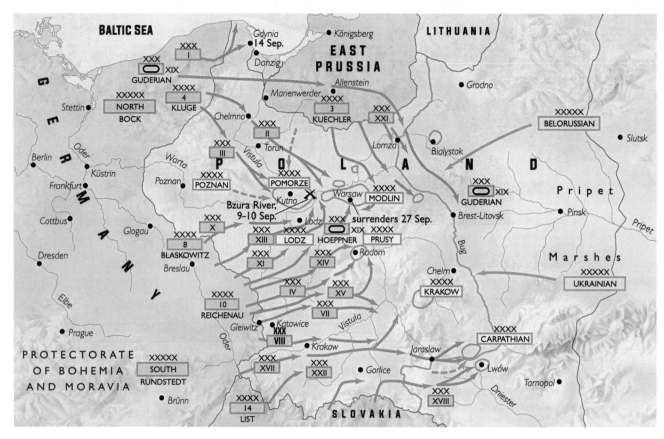

final Polish pockets of resistance   German-Soviet demarcation line, 30 September 1939

THE BOMBING OF WARSAW

As German forces closed in for the kill, the German Air Force was ordered to begin the bombing of Warsaw. The air force commander, Wolfram von Richthofen, cousin of the famous "Red Baron" First World War air ace, wanted to "completely eradicate" the Polish capital. On 22 September, 7,000 incendiaries set ablaze the Jewish ghetto; three days later a massive attack with 400 bombers destroyed or damaged 50 per cent of Warsaw's buildings for the loss of only three aircraft. Heavy smoke from the fires made it difficult to aim, and some bombs fell on German troops in the north of the city.

station at Gleiwitz on the night of 31 August–1 September was the signal. The order went out for the 1.5-million-strong German army, supported by more than 1,500 aircraft, to move forward in the first test of what came to be known as blitzkrieg or lightning war.

The German plan was for a two-pronged assault from East Prussia in the north and German Silesia in the south aimed towards the Polish capital, Warsaw. In the vanguard were five Panzer divisions of fast-moving mobile

OPPOSITE Poland 1939. German armies attacked Poland on 1 September 1939. The Soviet Red Army joined in the partition of Poland on 17 September. A demarcation line was agreed between the two armies on 28 September.

5 JANUARY 1939
Polish state visit to Berlin, Hitler demands the return of Danzig.

MARCH 1939
Polish Army draws up its plan for a Polish-German War.

22 MARCH 1939
Lithuania cedes city of Memel to Germany.

28 APRIL 1939
Hitler repudiates Anglo-German Naval Agreement.

28 APRIL 1939
German-Polish non-aggression pact of 1934 renounced by Hitler.

13 MAY 1939
Franco-Polish staff talks on military assistance begin.

25 AUGUST 1939
British–Polish treaty signed.

26 AUGUST 1939
German invasion postponed for five days.

German tanks and armoured vehicles cross a bridge over a river as they advance into Poland on 6 September 1939.

troops grouped around 300 tanks, supported by dive-bombers and fighters. It was the first time this new form of swift battlefield attack, using modern weaponry, had been tried out. The Polish army, almost one million strong, resisted bravely, but was overwhelmed by the Germans' striking power. The small Polish air force of around 400 planes was eliminated, though the German air force suffered 564 aircraft destroyed or damaged. Within a week of the start of the campaign German forces were 40–65km (25–40 miles) from Warsaw, tightening a noose around the encircled Polish armies. A final Polish stand was made at Warsaw and the fortress of Modlin to the north, but following the heavy bombing of the capital, Polish forces there surrendered on 27 September. Around 100,000 Polish soldiers escaped across neighbouring borders but 694,000 went into captivity. The German forces had lost some 13,000 men, the Poles 70,000: the first test of the rearmed German forces was a complete success.

The following day, 28 September, German and Soviet commanders met to decide the demarcation line between them. A new agreement was reached, the German-Soviet Treaty of Friendship, which sealed the partition of Poland, granting Warsaw to the area occupied by the Germans. Jews were victimized from the start and in November 1940 they were forced into a sealed ghetto in the city. Behind the German armies, Hitler had sent special "action squads" (Einsatzgruppen) manned by security agents and SS men, who began the systematic killing of all Polish intellectuals, nationalist politicians and government elite in a pattern that was to be repeated across Europe in the grim years of German occupation. By the end of the war, more than six million Poles, including three million Polish Jews, had been killed.

THE RED ARMY INVADES POLAND

On 17 September, Red Army forces began to roll across the Soviet-Polish border to occupy areas of eastern Poland agreed as the Soviet sphere of influence in the Molotov-Ribbentrop Pact. Stalin had been uncertain whether to act, but pressured by the Germans, he finally agreed. One million Soviet troops occupied the eastern provinces, and all Polish resistance ended by 28 September. Some 230,000 Polish troops went into Soviet captivity, including more than half the Polish officer corps, 5,000 of whom were taken to the forest of Katyn in April 1940 and murdered by a shot in the back of the neck. On 29 November, the Poles were officially made Soviet citizens.

Red Army tank and a German motorcycle troops on parade in Brest Litovsk, September 1939.

German troops raise a German flag over a ruin in the Westerplatte area of Danzig which surrendered on 7 September 1939.

HITLER'S ORDER NO. 1

Adolf Hitler's first War Directive, issued on 31 August 1939, orders the invasion of Poland. (See translation, page 156.)

Der Oberste Befehlshaber der Wehrmacht   Berlin, den 3 9 39.
OKW/WFA Nr. 170 /39 g.K.Chefs. L I

8 Ausfertigungen
2. Ausfertigung.

Weisung Nr. 1
für die Kriegführung.

1.) Nachdem alle politischen Möglichkeiten erschöpft sind, um
auf friedlichem Wege eine für Deutschland unerträgliche La-
ge an seiner Ostgrenze zu beseitigen, habe ich mich zur
gewaltsamen Lösung entschlossen.

2.) Der Angriff gegen Polen ist nach den für Fall Weiss getrof-
fenen Vorbereitungen zu führen mit den Abänderungen, die
sich beim Heer durch den inzwischen fast vollendeten Auf-
marsch ergeben.

Aufgabenverteilung und Operationsziel bleiben unver-
ändert.

Angriffstag:.1.9.39..

Angriffszeit ....

Diese Zeit gilt auch für die Unternehmungen Gdingen -
Danziger Bucht und Brücke Dirschau.

3.) Im Westen kommt es darauf an, die Verantwortung für die Er-
öffnung von Feindseligkeiten eindeutig England und Frankreich zu überlassen. Geringfügigen Grenzverletzungen ist
zunächst rein örtlich entgegen zu treten.

Die von uns Holland, Belgien, Luxemburg und der
Schweiz zugesicherte Neutralität ist peinlich zu achten.

- 2 -

- 2 -

Die deutsche Westgrenze ist zu Lande an keiner Stelle
ohne meine ausdrückliche Genehmigung zu überschreiten.

Zur See gilt das gleiche für alle kriegerischen oder
als solche zu deutenden Handlungen.

Die defensiven Massnahmen der Luftwaffe sind zunächst auf die unbedingte Abwehr feindl. Luftangriffe an
der Reichsgrenze zu beschränken, wobei so lange als mög-
lich die Grenze der neutralen Staaten bei der Abwehr einzel-
ner Flugzeuge und kleinerer Einheiten zu achten ist.
Erst wenn beim Einsatz stärkerer franz. und engl. Angriffs-
verbände über die neutralen Staaten gegen deutsches Gebiet die Luftverteidigung im Westen nicht mehr gesichert
ist, ist die Abwehr auch über diesem neutralen Gebiet frei-
zugeben.

Schnellste Orientierung des OKW über jede Verletzung
der Neutralität dritter Staaten durch die Westgegner ist
besonders wichtig.

4.) Eröffnen England und Frankreich die Feindseligkeiten
gegen Deutschland, so ist es Aufgabe der im Westen ope-
rierenden Teile der Wehrmacht, unter möglichster Schonung
der Kräfte die Voraussetzungen für den siegreichen Ab-
schluss der Operationen gegen Polen zu erhalten. Im Rah-
men dieser Aufgabe sind die feindl. Streitkräfte und deren wehrwirtschaftl. Kraftquellen nach Kräften zu schädi-
gen. Den Befehl zum Beginn von Angriffshandlungen behalte
ich mir in jedem Fall vor.

- 3 -

Das <u>Heer</u> hält den Westwall und trifft Vorbereitungen, dessen Umfassung im Norden - unter Verletzung belg.
oder holländ. Gebietes durch die Westmächte - zu verhindern. Rücken franz. Kräfte in Luxemburg ein, so bleibt
die Sprengung der Grenzbrücken freigegeben.

Die <u>Kriegsmarine</u> führt Handelskrieg mit dem Schwer-
punkt gegen England. Zur Verstärkung der Wirkung kann
mit der Erklärung von Gefahrenzonen gerechnet werden.
OKM meldet, in welchen Seegebieten und in welchem Umfang
Gefahrenzonen für zweckmässig gehalten werden. Der Wort-
laut für eine öffentl. Erklärung ist im Benehmen mit dem
Ausw. Amte vorzubereiten und mir über OKW zur Genehmigung vorzulegen.

Die Ostsee ist gegen feindl. Einbruch zu sichern.
Die Entscheidung, ob zu diesem Zwecke die Ostsee-Eingänge
mit Minen gesperrt werden dürfen, ~~bleibt vorbehalten.~~
trifft Ob.d.M.

Die <u>Luftwaffe</u> hat in erster Linie den Einsatz der
franz. und engl. Luftwaffe gegen das deutsche Heer und
den deutschen Lebensraum zu verhindern.

Bei der Kampfführung gegen England ist der Einsatz
der Luftwaffe zur Störung der engl. Seezufuhr, der
Rüstungsindustrie, der Truppentransporte nach Frankreich
vorzubereiten. Günstige Gelegenheit zu einem wirkungs-
vollen Angriff gegen massierte engl. Flotteneinheiten,
insbes. gegen Schlachtschiffe und Flugzeugträger ist aus-

zunutzen. Angriffe gegen London bleiben meiner Entscheidung vorbehalten.

Die Angriffe gegen das engl. Mutterland sind unter
dem Gesichtspunkt vorzubereiten, dass unzureichender Er-
folg mit Teilkräften unter allen Umständen zu vermeiden
ist.

Verteiler:

OKH	1w Ausf.
OKM	2. "
R.d.L.u.Ob.d.L.	3. "
OKW:	
Chef WFA	4. "
L	5.-8. "

3 SEPTEMBER 1939

BRITAIN AND FRANCE DECLARE WAR

At 11.15 on Sunday morning, 3 September 1939, the British Prime Minister announced over the radio from 10 Downing Street that Britain was once again at war with Germany. No sooner had he finished speaking than the air-raid sirens set up in the capital let out their mournful wailing. All over southern England people dived for bunkers, cellars or doorways. Neville Chamberlain was reluctant to leave his office but was finally persuaded to go down into the shelter prepared for him. It turned out to be a false alarm, but the initial panic reflected the profound fear that the new war would be won or lost by bombing with gas, germ warfare and fire.

Britain's decision to go to war was almost inevitable once German forces had crossed the Polish frontier. As early as February, Chamberlain had pledged Britain to defend France, and from March the British and French military worked on a war plan so that they could make advance preparations. They expected to face a three-year war of attrition, a repeat of the First World War in which German resistance would be sapped by economic blockade, food shortages and, if necessary, the bombing of German cities. In France, opinion rallied to the idea of confronting fascism, though right-wing groups stuck posters up on the walls of Paris asking "Who Will Die for Danzig?". By August, Britain and France were mobilizing, ration books were already being distributed to local authorities and millions of children and mothers prepared for evacuation away from the threatened cities. The British public steeled itself for the coming conflict "like the glassy sea when a hurricane comes", wrote the journalist Malcolm Muggeridge. Intelligence sources confirmed that German armies were moving into position. Although the British and French governments promised to help the Poles when war came, they

6 FEBRUARY 1939
Chamberlain pledges in House of Commons to support France militarily.

13 FEBRUARY 1939
Joint Anglo-French military staff talks begin.

14 AUGUST 1939
Franco-British delegation arrives for talks in Moscow on possible Three-Power Pact.

5 SEPTEMBER 1939
Roosevelt declares an embargo on arms sales to the fighting powers.

NEVILLE CHAMBERLAIN
(1869–1940)

Born into a family of Birmingham screw manufacturers, Neville Chamberlain was a hard-working and successful politician in home affairs but is remembered as a failure in foreign policy because of his attempt to "appease" the dictators in the 1930s. A Conservative politician, he made his reputation as a reforming Minister of Health in the 1920s and a successful Chancellor of the Exchequer in 1931–37, steering the British economy out of the slump. He became prime minister in May 1937, and tried to secure a "grand settlement" of European affairs in order to avoid the threat of a second world war. In 1939, he came to realize that Hitler could never be satisfied with concessions and prepared for war. His reputation suffered from not confronting Hitler sooner, but he was always sincere in his strong desire for peace.

Neville Chamberlain broadcasting to the nation. He was an early enthusiast for radio and newsreel talks, and announced the state of war over the radio on 3 September 1939.

privately agreed that assistance was useless and made no plans to do so. They hoped to restore a free Poland when the war was over and planned to hold tight on the western front.

In the last days before war there was a sudden flurry of activity. A Swedish businessman and friend of Hermann Göring, Birger Dahlerus, was despatched to London to see if the British could be separated from France by negotiating a deal. His mission was a blind, intended to confuse the British while Germany attacked Poland. At the last minute, after the

German attack, Mussolini tried to intervene as he had at Munich, but the British and French governments, though willing to consider sensible proposals, were not prepared to allow Germany to occupy Poland. An ultimatum was delivered to Germany at 9 a.m. on 3 September by the British Ambassador, Sir Nevile Henderson, who found no one at the German Foreign Office except for Hitler's interpreter, Paul Schmidt, to whom he gave the solemn document. Schmidt hurried over to the Reich chancellery to read the ultimatum to a silent Hitler, who at the

Crowds watch as cabinet ministers pose for photographs outside 10 Downing Street on the day Britain declared war.

21

EVACUATION

Preparations were made before the outbreak of war in Britain, France and Germany for the mass evacuation of children and mothers from the vulnerable major cities. In Britain, official programmes covered evacuation of 1.75 million, with two million more expected to arrange private evacuation. Over 100,000 volunteers helped to organize the exodus and reception of the evacuees.

The plan was activated on 1 September 1939 but only 40 per cent of those eligible took up the opportunity and 60 per cent of these had returned home by January 1940. In Germany hundreds of thousands were moved from the frontier zone after 3 September, but there too most had returned home by the start of 1940.

end turned to his Foreign Minister von Ribbentrop and asked in harsh tones, "What now?" War could no longer be avoided. Chamberlain and the French premier, Edouard Daladier, would both have preferred peace, but could not abandon their commitment to Poland and to each other. The British ultimatum ran out at 11 a.m., the French later, at 5.00 p.m., and India, Australia and New Zealand declared war the same day. South Africa and Canada followed shortly after, on 6 and 10 September respectively. In France, six million men were in the process of mobilization. The American Ambassador watched French troops leaving Paris: "The men left in silence. There were no bands, no songs," but only "self-control and a quiet courage".

OPPOSITE Londoners run for shelter minutes after the British declaration of war on 3 September, when the first (false) air-raid alarm was sounded.

GERMANY INVADES IN THE WEST

On 10 May 1940 German forces launched a series of swift operations against the Dutch, Belgian and French armed forces. Hitler had wanted to invade in the West in November 1939 but bad weather prevented it. During the spring, German military planners prepared a campaign based on a rapid defeat of Allied forces by striking with armour and aircraft through the heavily wooded Ardennes sector of the front, where the French Maginot Line fortifications were weakest. The balance of forces between the two sides favoured the Western Allies in army divisions (144 to 141), artillery pieces (13,974 to 7,378) and tanks (3,384 to 2,445); German fighter and bomber forces were outnumbered on paper by the Allies (3,254 to 3,562), but both the French and the British chose to keep large air forces away from the battlefield, defending the rest of France and mainland Britain.

The rapid German advance was based on a number of daring strategic strokes and the miscalculation of the Allies. The Western plan was based on a rapid movement of forces into Belgium and the Netherlands to counter the expected German attack. After German forces attacked the Netherlands and seized the key Belgian fortress of Eben Emael with the first successful airborne assault on 10 May, the Allies attempted to move forces into the Low Countries to halt the German advance. Dutch resistance crumbled and within a few days Belgian, British and French forces were in retreat. Unknown to the Western Allies, large German formations of armoured divisions, heavily protected by fighters, had by 12 May mustered in the Ardennes forest, considered virtually impassable by the French High Command, and stood poised for an historic breakthrough.

Under the command of General von Kleist, Guderian's Panzer divisions broke across the Meuse River on 13 May and, heavily supported by the Junkers Ju 87 dive bomber and large numbers of medium bombers, unhinged the whole French front by driving a powerful wedge between two French armies, General Hutziger's 2nd and General Corap's 9th. "There has been a rather serious hitch at Sedan," reported Colonel Lacaille, chief-of-staff of the 2nd Army. The "hitch" turned into a rout. The French front collapsed and German commanders began the successful rush for the coast in the hope of encircling and destroying all the remaining Allied armies in the pocket. By 19 May Guderian's tanks had reached the Channel coast at Abbeville. A small number of counterattacks by French and British forces held up what was close to becoming a foregone

The Junkers Ju 87B "Stuka" was the most famous of the German dive bombers and used to devasting effect during Germany's Blitzkrieg of the West. However, as learned during the Battle of Britain, it required total air superiority to be effective as it was slow and cumbersome.

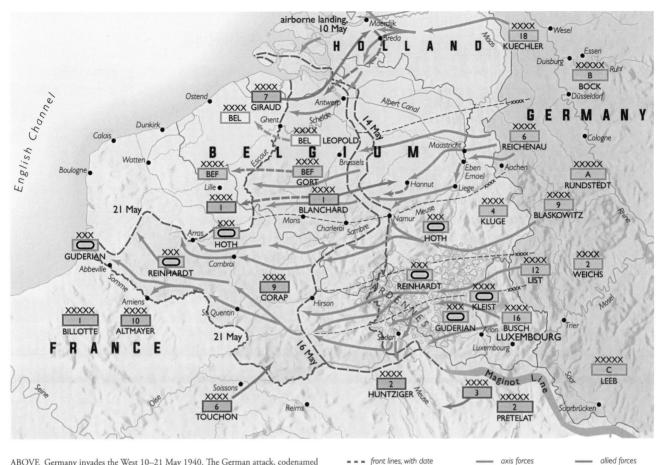

ABOVE Germany invades the West 10–21 May 1940. The German attack, codenamed Operation "Sichelschnitt" (Sicklestroke), was the brainchild of General von Manstein and Hitler's preferred route into western Europe.

- - - front lines, with date   ───── axis forces   ───── allied forces

GENERAL MAURICE-GUSTAVE GAMELIN
(1872–1958)

Often regarded as the commander who lost the Battle of France in 1940, General Gamelin was in fact a successful and innovative soldier who helped to modernise the French army in the 1930s and prepare it for the conflict with Germany. He was commander-in-chief of French forces in May 1940 when the Germans invaded. His plan to move French mobile forces rapidly into the Netherlands to stop the German advance fatally weakened the French line opposite the axis of German advance. He was sacked on 19 May as the Allied front crumbled.

conclusion. On 28 May, after a brave defence of western Belgium, the Belgian king surrendered; the Netherlands had capitulated on 14 May, following a fierce air bomb attack on the Dutch port of Rotterdam.

The rapid German advance created panic in the French leadership. British reinforcements were slow to arrive and the bulk of British air power remained in Britain to defend against a possible German air assault. On 16 May Winston Churchill flew to Paris where he was told that there was no French reserve left to hold up the German advance. The same day the French premier, Paul Reynaud, told the French parliament that only a miracle could save France from defeat. As the noose tightened around the trapped British and French forces in northern France, plans were made to try to hold the line of the River Somme, where more than 20 years before some of the bloodiest battles of the First World War had been fought. On 23 May the British military Chiefs-of-Staff decided that the war in France was lost and prepared to abandon their ally. On 26 May British forces began to evacuate from the northern French port of Dunkirk. France was forced to fight on alone.

15 JANUARY 1940

Belgian government refuses permission for Allied forces to enter Belgian territory.

10 MAY 1940

Winston Churchill becomes Prime Minister of Great Britain following the resignation of Neville Chamberlain.

10 MAY 1940

British troops occupy Iceland to prevent the Germans from using it as a base from which to attack Allied convoys.

11 MAY 1940

Luxembourg occupied by German troops.

26 MAY 1940

A German aerial attack sinks the British cruiser *Curlew* off the coast of Norway.

GENERAL HEINZ GUDERIAN
(1888–1954)

German officer who in the 1930s pioneered fast mobile warfare spearheaded by the use of armour, the famous Blitzkrieg strategy. He was Commander of Mobile Troops by the late 1930s, and led the 19th Panzer Corps during the invasions of Poland and France, where his forces played a critical part in the breakthrough at Sedan which opened up the French front. He won spectacular victories in the Russian campaign in 1941, but fell out with Hitler, who sacked him in December. He was appointed Inspector-General of Armoured Troops in 1943, then Chief of Army Staff until Hitler dismissed him again in March 1945.

ABOVE General Rommel, Commander of 7th Panzer Division, and his staff, plot their way through France, May 1940. They were known as the "Ghost Division" due to the speed with which they attacked.

OPPOSITE A mother leads her children to safety having been made homeless by a German attack, Belgium, May 1940.

26 MAY–4 JUNE 1940

DUNKIRK

As German forces pressed forward into France they opened up a wide gap between the British Expeditionary Force in northern France and the bulk of the French army to the south. By the fourth week of May, German thrusts had also separated the BEF from the crumbling Belgian army, which capitulated three days later. There existed a very real danger that the entire British force would be encircled and captured, but on 23 May von Runstedt halted the armoured forces, and the following day Hitler, uncertain about the strength of the French army to the south, concurred. The German armour stopped in front of a network of water-courses surrounding the area around Lille and Dunkirk now occupied by the BEF and a substantial number of trapped French divisions. This pause allowed a rough perimeter defence to be established by the Allies. On 26 May, the British government ordered Lord Gort, the BEF commander, to evacuate as many troops as he could from France. The evacuation was masterminded by Vice Admiral Bertram Ramsay, who later, as Naval Commander, organized the shipping for the D-Day invasion. Given the codename Operation "Dynamo" – after the small dynamo room in the Dover cliffs used as the operational base – the saving of the BEF became one of the great legends in Britain's war effort.

British forces line up on the beach at Dunkirk waiting to be evacuated.

The fighting retreat begun around 21 May was among the fiercest action of the campaign. The troops holding the British line at Arras were ordered to "fight to the last man and the last round". When German attacks resumed on 26 May, every mile of ground was contested. Under a hail of bombs from German aircraft, an estimated 850–950 small ships and larger naval and merchant vessels plied back and forth, carrying British troops between Dunkirk and the southern British ports. In addition to Royal Navy vessels and large steamers, there came lifeboats and trawlers. The Port of London Authority sent nine tugs drawing barges behind them. Fortunately, British fighter aircraft were able to reach Dunkirk from British bases and kept up regular sorties against German units, though around 100 British fighters were lost. When the weather was clear, German aircraft exacted a heavy toll: on 1 June, three destroyers were sunk and Ramsay ordered sailings only at night.

During the eight days of the evacuation, an estimated 338,000 troops were rescued including 110,000 French servicemen, most of whom were

BELOW Motor vehicles on the quayside at Cherbourg during the evacuation, 13 June 1940.

RIGHT Officers of the Royal Ulster Rifles awaiting evacuation at Bray Dunes, about 8 kilometres (5 miles) from Dunkirk.

THE OTHER DUNKIRKS

Even as Operation "Dynamo" ended, there were more than 100,000 British troops still stationed in northern France, and as French resistance crumbled they fell back on the ports. On 13 June, 11,200 men were evacuated from Le Havre on the north French coast; 27,000 from St Nazaire on 17–18 June. In total around 273,000 more British, French and Polish soldiers and airmen were evacuated to Britain between 13 and 25 June, a total not far short of the number saved at Dunkirk. On 17 June, a single German plane succeeded in hitting the overcrowded *Lancastria* in St Nazaire harbour. The ship keeled over and only 2,477 of an estimated 6,000 crew and evacuees were saved. This was the worst disaster in British maritime history.

20 MAY 1940

German army reaches the Channel coast of France.

26 MAY 1940

Operation "Dynamo" officially launched to evacuate British soldiers from France.

27 MAY 1940

Surrender of Calais.

3 JUNE 1940

German air force launches a bombing attack on Paris killing 250.

4 JUNE 1940

Last evacuation from Dunkirk.

19 JUNE 1940

Evacuation of French and Polish soldiers from south-western France.

saved only on the last two days after Ramsay was ordered to send back the big ships to rescue non-British forces as well. A mixture of British and French units continued to defend the pocket, and for many of them, including the 51st Highland Division, forced to surrender in mid-June, evacuation was not possible. Some 8,000 British soldiers went into captivity. On the evacuation beaches discipline was hard to maintain and panicking soldiers were sometimes killed or beaten to keep order, while British forces also shot French soldiers suspected of spying or betrayal. On 27 May, a group of the Royal Norfolks was caught by the SS "Death's Head" Division, commanded by General Theodor Eicke, former commandant of Dachau, and 97 of them were murdered in cold blood.

The Dunkirk evacuation was both a victory and a defeat. It showed how important British naval power was and it also provided a taste of the conflict between the two air forces that later dominated the summer and autumn of 1940. German aircraft losses during the Battle of France were higher than in the later Battle of Britain. Yet Dunkirk did mean an ignominious end to Allied efforts to defeat Germany on land. Almost all the British army's equipment was abandoned or destroyed, and a new army had to be rebuilt over the course of the following years. "Wars are not won", Churchill remarked on 4 June, "by evacuations".

ABOVE French soldiers captured when the German army entered Dunkirk after the British evacuation, 4 June 1940.

FIELD MARSHAL VISCOUNT GORT, VC
(1886–1946)

John Standish Vereker, Viscount Gort, was born into an Irish aristocratic family. He served in the Grenadier Guards and became a battalion commander in 1917. After a long army career, he was appointed Chief of the Imperial General Staff in 1937. He held that office until September 1939, when he was sent to France to command the British Expeditionary Force, where he was responsible for organizing the evacuation from Dunkirk. He later became Governor of Malta during the siege of the island, and was created a Field Marshal in 1943.

Troops arrive back at Dover from Dunkirk, 31 May 1940. In total around 228,000 British forces were rescued in nine days.

4–17 JUNE 1940

THE FALL OF FRANCE

The surrender of Belgium and the British evacuation from Dunkirk left France fighting almost alone against the German advance. General Maxime Weygand, who succeeded General Gamelin on 19 May, organized an improvised defensive line along two rivers, the Somme and the Aisne, which had witnessed much of the fighting in the First World War. The German army reorganized into two major armoured spearheads led by von Kleist and Guderian, and attacked the Weygand Line on 5 and 9 June. After a few days of fierce fighting, the German forces reached the eastern edge of Paris. The capital was declared an open city, and on 14 June the German army entered almost deserted streets. The French government had fled first to Tours, where Churchill flew on 11 June to try to rally French resistance, then to Bordeaux. In the days before the German arrival, thousands of Parisians fled by car, train or on foot in what became known as l'exode – "the exodus".

Following the breakthrough to Paris, resistance began to crumble despite the existence of large units of the French army and substantial numbers of aircraft not yet defeated. German armoured forces pushed forward at high speed, reaching Brest on the Atlantic coast by 19 June, Nantes by 20 June and as far as Bordeaux by 25 June, when the armistice, sought by the French government on 17 June and signed five days later, finally came into effect. In the east of France, the Maginot Line was penetrated in several places while

German forces swung south to encircle what was left of the Second French Army Group under General Prételat. French forces were forced to surrender piecemeal, but by 22 June French resistance towards the Germans was over.

On the Italian-French frontier in the south, however, hostilities continued. Mussolini declared war on France and Britain on 10 June, anxious not to miss any advantages he might gain from a peace settlement. Eleven days later, the 22 Italian divisions on the Italian-French frontier,

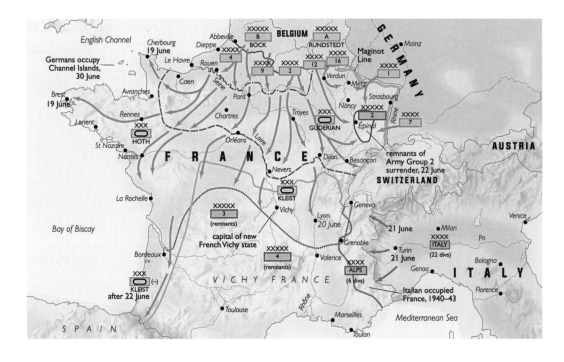

LEFT The fall of France, 5–25 June 1940. From 5 June the German armies rolled across France, reaching Paris on 14 June and the Atlantic coast by 19 June. The armistice left southern France under the control of a government at Vichy. Italian forces occupied a region of south-eastern France.

Front lines

—— 5 June

—·— 13 June

—— 17 June

···· armistice line, 22 June

—— boundary between German occupied and Vichy France

French infantry surrender to the advancing German army in June 1940. Hundreds of thousands of French POWs were later made to work for the German war effort.

totalling 300,000 men, were used to attack the southern French defences where they were held up by only six French divisions of approximately 85,000; the French strength had been greatly reduced following the redeployment of General Olry's forces to the north to face the German threat there. After four days of fighting, the Italians had gained almost nothing in the face of entrenched defences in difficult terrain. The Italian forces lost 1,258 dead and 2,631 wounded in the campaign; only 20 French soldiers were killed, and 84 wounded. On 24 June, an armistice was signed, ending what had been a brief, pointless and inglorious campaign. The battle to the north cost the French an estimated 90,000 dead and the loss of 1.9 million men as prisoners of war; German losses were 29,640 dead and 163,000 wounded.

For other Frenchmen the war continued beyond the armistice. On 6 June, the French premier, Paul Reynaud, had appointed the young

10 JUNE 1940

Italy declares war on France and Britain.

14 JUNE 1940

Paris falls to the German army.

16 JUNE 1940

Premier Paul Reynaud resigns.

19 JUNE 1940

German army reaches Atlantic coast at Brest.

20 JUNE 1940

Japan forces France to agree to Japanese naval vessels in Indo-China.

1 JULY 1940

French parliament votes Marshal Pétain special powers, bringing the Third Republic to an end.

MARSHAL PHILIPPE PÉTAIN
(1856–1951)

To many Frenchmen Marshal Pétain was both a hero and a villain. In the First World War he commanded the defence of the French fortress of Verdun and was hailed in 1918 as one of the victors over Germany, for which he was rewarded with the title Marshal of France. In 1940, the ageing hero, who had been ambassador in Spain in the 1930s and from May 1940 vice-premier, was called upon to bolster French morale in the crisis weeks of June 1940. On 16 June, as French resistance collapsed, he became prime minister and called for an armistice. He established a new authoritarian government in the small town of Vichy in central France, from which his regime took its name. He was forced to collaborate with the Germans, including in the campaign against the Jews, and at the end of the war he was arrested and later sentenced to death. He died in captivity on the Île d'Yeu.

Hitler standing at the Trocadero in Paris, in front of the
Eiffel Tower, during his only visit to the captured city,
on 28 June 1940. He was said to be delighted that Paris
had been surrendered with its architecture undamaged
by bombing.

General Charles de Gaulle as Under Secretary for War. He wanted to continue the fight, and on 16 June encouraged Churchill to offer France a union of the two countries, which he did with the backing of his cabinet. The French government refused, but de Gaulle smuggled himself out of France in an RAF aircraft, and in London on 18 June made an historic appeal to a "Free France" to continue the fight against the German enemy. De Gaulle and the small number of supporters he gathered in England formally established the Free French forces on 7 August; they numbered only 2,240 officers and men. The newly formed Vichy government of Marshal Pétain declared them to be traitors but they formed the nucleus of what was to become a large and effective fighting force later in the war.

THE CARRIAGE AT COMPIÈGNE

Nothing so symbolized German humiliation at the end of the First World War as the railway carriage in the small French town of Compiègne where German delegates were compelled to sign the armistice that ended hostilities on 11 November 1918. When Marshal Pétain asked for an armistice from the Germans on 17 June, Hitler insisted that it should be signed in the same place as in 1918. The French General Charles Huntziger led a delegation to meet Hitler on 21 June, and the armistice was signed the following day in the railway carriage. Its 24 articles were dictated by the German side rather than negotiated. The armistice came into force on 25 June following a second armistice signing in Rome to bring Italian-French hostilities to a close.

German troops parade through Paris following the occupation of the French capital, which was declared an open city on 13 June 1940 to avoid bombing attacks.

CHURCHILL'S "FINEST HOUR" SPEECH

Notes for Winston Churchill's historic speech of 18 June 1940 announcing an end to the Battle of France and the onset of the Battle of Britain. The red annotations were typical of Churchill, who often used a red crayon.

23

```
The House will hv read the historic
    declaration in which at the desire
    of many Frenchmen,
        and of our own hearts,
        we hv proclaimed our willingness
            to conclude at the darkest
            hour in French history,
            a Union of common
                citizenship in their
                            struggle.

However matters may go in France,
    or with the French Govt.
    we in this Island and in the
    British Empire,
        will never lose our sense of
            comradeship with the French
                        people.

If we are now called upon to endure
    what they hv suffered,
        we shall emulate their courage,
        and if final victory rewards our
                                    toils,
            they shall share the gain,——
            aye, and freedom shall be
                restored to all.

We abate nothing of our just demands.

Czechs, Poles, Norwegians, Dutch and
    Belgians, who have joined their
                causes with our own.
                All shall be restored
What General Weygand calls 'the battle
    of France' is over.

The battle of Britain is about to
                        begin.
```

24

```
Upon this battle depends the
    survival of Christian civilization.

Upon it depends our own British life
    and the long continuity of our
    institutions, and our Empire.

The whole fury and might of the enemy
    must very soon be turned on us.
                            he
Hitler knows that we will hv to break
    us in this Island, or lose the war.

If we can stand up to him,
    all Europe may be freed,
        and the life of the world
        may move forward into the
            broad and sunlit uplands.

But if we fail,
    then the whole world,
        including the United States,
        and all that we have known and
                                cared for,
            will sink into the abyss of a
            new Dark Age
                made more sinister and
                perhaps more prolonged by
                    the lights of perverted
                        Science.

Let us therefore brace ourselves to
    our duty, and so bear ourselves that
        if the British Empire and
        Commonwealth lasts for a
            thousand years, men will still
                say,

'This was their finest hour'.
```

S E C R E T. F/LT.FORBES. FORM F

COMBAT REPORT.

Sector Serial No. .... (A) ....

Serial No. of Order detailing Flight or Squadron to Patrol .... (B) ....

Date .... (C) ..... 7/9/40 ....

Flight, Squadron .... (D) Flight : B Sqdn. : 303 Polish

Number of Enemy Aircraft .... (E) ..... 40 DO 215 & 50 ME 109 ....

Type of Enemy Aircraft .... (F) ..... Bombers & Fighters ......

Time Attack was delivered .... (G) ..... 1700 ....

Place Attack was delivered .... (H) ..... Essex ....

Height of Enemy .... (J) ..... 20,000 ft. ....

Enemy Casualties .... (K) ..... 1 DO 215 ....

Our Casualties .... Aircraft ..... (L) ..... 1 Hurricane Cat.2 ....

Personnel ..... (M) ..... Pilot slightly wounded.

GENERAL REPORT .... (R)

We were ordered into the air to rendez-vous with No.1 Squadron who took off first. We were sent up 15,000 ft and then to 20,000 ft and proceeded North and then East. No.1 Squadron remained below us to Starboard and in front. I led the Squadron up to 24000 ft, determined after my experience yesterday not to be caught napping at too low an altitude. It is easy to get down to the enemy and impossible to attack climbing when the slow speed makes one an easy prey to the ME 109's. I sighted a formation of about 40 enemy bombers flying Northwards. Their rearguard of ME 109's were engaged with Spitfires at 25,000 & 30,000 ft. No.1 Squadron went in to attack the enemy's tail and drew off most of the remaining fighter escort. It was a perfect combination of circumstances. We were flying in Vics line astern. The enemy was flying also in Vics line astern with 3 and 5 A/C in each Vic. The A A fire had loosened their formations. As soon as No.1 Squadron attacked, the enemy wheeled Eastwards, and we caught them on the turn. We reformed towards the enemy and launched the attack in Vics abrest, striking the formation a little to the rear of centre. They were easy meat. We came at them from partially up sun and at great speed as they turned away from us. I led in, and attacked a DO 215, hitting the starboard wing. Great chunks fell off the wing and engine, which stopped. I gave another good burst into the cockpit and more stuff fell off. E/A fell away sideways in a long glide and hit the sea. I broke away, and whilst in a steep turn, a shell hit my starboard wing root and exploded. I felt my leg was wounded and there were 3 or 4 glycol and hydraulic system leaks in the cockpit. I decided to return to an Aerodrome and get the machine down whole. I succeeded in regaining Northolt and landing without mishap.

Signature

	Section	Forbes F/Lt.
O.C.	Flight	Blue 1
	Squadron	B
		303 Squadron No. Polish.

(3567—1611) Wt. 27885—2553 850 Pads 9/39 T.S. 700 FORM 1151

THE BATTLE OF BRITAIN

On 18 June 1940, Winston Churchill told the House of Commons that "the Battle of France is over. I expect the Battle of Britain is about to begin". Over the following four months, the German air force attempted to destroy the RAF and undermine British military capability to an extent that would make the German invasion of southern England a possibility. It was the aerial duel fought out over the southern counties of Britain that became the Battle of Britain.

There were no clear dates for when the battle started and ended, but after it was over, an official Air Ministry pamphlet dated it from 8 August, when the air assault began to intensify, and ended it on 31 October, when air attacks by German fighters petered out. German attacks began on 5–6

June, before the final defeat of France, and continued intermittently over June and July. These were probing attacks designed to lure Britain's RAF Fighter Command into combat and to destroy ports and communications. Only in August did the German air force commander-in-chief Hermann

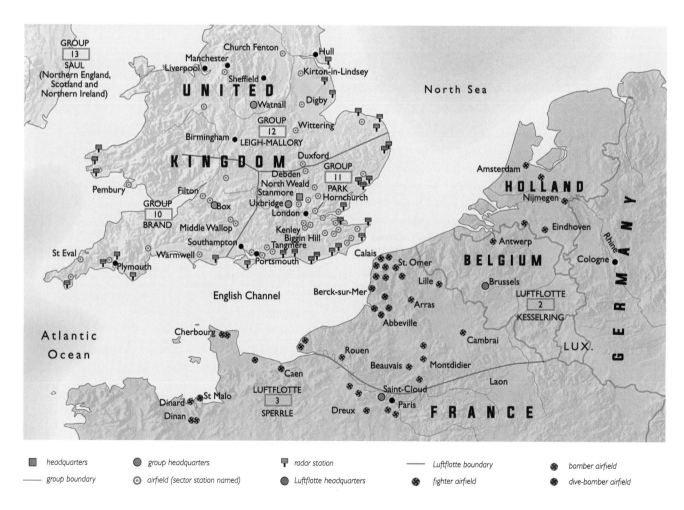

headquarters   **group headquarters**   **radar station**   ------ Luftflotte boundary   **bomber airfield**

------ group boundary   **airfield (sector station named)**   **Luftflotte headquarters**   **fighter airfield**   **dive-bomber airfield**

When the approach of enemy planes was reported, RAF squadrons were "scrambled" to intercept them. Here pilots of No.19 Squadron, based at Fowlmere in Cambridgeshire, pose for a photographer by their waiting aircraft at the height of the battle.

Göring order an intensified campaign following Hitler's directive, issued on 1 August, "to overpower the English air force". Air Fleet 2, under the command of General Albert Kesselring, and Air Fleet 3, commanded by General Hugo Sperrle, began a sustained attack on the airfields, supply depots and radar stations in southern England. By mid August, Göring was confident that Fighter Command was on its knees and he ordered a final blow. The main attack was scheduled for Eagle Day (Adlertag) on 13 August, though poor weather on that day blunted the full scale of the assault. Between 12 August and 6 September there were 53 main attacks on airfields, all but two of them against the bases of No. 11 Group led by Air Vice-Marshal Keith Park. The raids against radar stations were not sustained and only three of Park's airfields were put out of action, and then only temporarily.

The German side assumed that the RAF was close to extinction, but the reality was very different. On 23 August, Fighter Command had an operational strength of 672 Spitfire and Hurricane fighters; by early September the figure was 738, more than at the start of the battle. Fighter Command losses totalled 444 aircraft between 6 August and 2 September; German losses were over 900 for the whole month, including bomber aircraft. Great attention had been paid by the commander-in-chief of Fighter Command, Air Marshal Hugh Dowding, to conserving RAF

4 JULY 1940
German air force begins attacks on Channel convoys.

17 JULY 1940
Britain closes the Burma Road supply route to appease Japanese.

3 AUGUST 1940
Italian armies invade British Somaliland.

13 AUGUST 1940
"Eagle Day" launches the German attack of airfields.

25–26 AUGUST 1940
The RAF bombs Berlin.

27 AUGUST 1940
US Congress approves conscription by a majority of one vote.

2 SEPTEMBER 1940
"Destroyers for bases" deal signed with the US.

4 SEPTEMBER 1940
Hitler announces switch to bombing cities.

7 SEPTEMBER 1940
The German Blitz on Britain begins.

15 SEPTEMBER 1940
Major German attack on London with high civilian casualties.

strength, training pilots and building reserves. Though hard-pressed in August and September, Fighter Command never came close to collapse. As the battle went on, it was the German air force that suffered levels of loss of aircraft and pilots that became in the end impossible to sustain. When Winston Churchill famously told the House of Commons on 20 August that "never in the field of human conflict was so much owed by so many to so few," he disguised the reality of a rising graph of British aircraft and pilot supply.

At the beginning of September, there came a sudden change in German tactics. The attack on the RAF was much reduced and German bomber fleets, escorted by large numbers of Messerschmitt Me109 fighters, were directed to attack London and other urban centres. Although the switch is often attributed to Hitler's desire to get revenge for RAF attacks on Berlin on the night of 25–26 August, it had already been planned on the assumption that Fighter Command had been destroyed. On 2 September, Göring ordered phase two of the attack, to destroy Britain's military and economic capability and demoralize the population prior to invasion. Hitler's speech on 4 September promising revenge was a propaganda stunt designed to make it look as if Britain had started the bombing. The switch in emphasis suited Fighter Command. It was now possible to attack the bombers as they approached London in large numbers and on their return, while German fighters were tied to protecting the slower and more vulnerable bombers and so less free to combat British fighters. In the first week of attacks, the German air force lost 298 aircraft, with 60 losses on 15 September, the day that has been celebrated ever since as Battle of Britain Day. Thanks to the survival of the radar chain, there was always advance warning of attack. British tactics were designed to maximize the damage to the attacking force and by the end of September it was clear to German commanders that they could not maintain the levels of attrition they were suffering. At the cost of only 443 pilots, Fighter Command inflicted losses of 1,733 aircraft on the German air force for the loss of 915 of their own. The conflict has gone down in British history alongside the defeat of the Spanish Armada in 1588 as one of the legendary moments in Britain's military past.

AIR VICE-MARSHAL SIR KEITH PARK
(1892–1975)

One of the key roles during the Battle of Britain was played by the New Zealand airman Air Vice-Marshal Keith Park, who commanded No. 11 Group, Fighter Command, in south-eastern England. An artillery officer in the Great War, he was wounded at the Battle of the Somme and subsequently joined the Royal Flying Corps. After 1918, he became a career RAF officer and in 1940 was posted to command No. 11 Group. His squadrons organized the air defence of the Dunkirk pocket, and then took the brunt of the German attack in the autumn of 1940. Park was a shrewd tactician who watched German operations carefully and adjusted the tactics of his own force to maximize the damage done to incoming German aircraft. His flexibility and tactical imagination were vital qualities in winning the air battle. He was later posted as air officer commanding Malta in 1942, where he organised the air defence of the island, and ended up as Allied air commander, south-east Asia, in 1945.

ABOVE Interior of the Sector "G" Operations Room at the RAF base at Duxford, Cambridgeshire, September 1940. The callsigns of the squadrons operating out of Duxford are visible on the wall behind the operator third from left. On the extreme right are the radio operators in direct contact with the aircraft.

OPERATION "SEALION"

The defeat of France and the expulsion of British forces from mainland Europe presented Hitler with a quite unexpected opportunity. German leaders assumed that Britain would see sense and find a way to end a conflict that could no longer be won. "We are very close to the end of the war," Joseph Goebbels, Hitler's Propaganda Minister, told his staff on 23 June. Hitler preferred a political solution and thought the idea of an invasion of Britain "very hazardous", but he decided in early July to explore both possibilities. On 7 July, the armed forces were instructed to begin preliminary planning for a possible invasion, and on 16 July Hitler finally approved War Directive 16 for Operation "Sealion", the invasion of the south-eastern coast of England. This was to be a last resort if a political solution could not be found. On 19 July, Hitler made a peace offer in the German Reichstag. The speech was a celebration of German victory and Hitler made it clear that he would discuss terms "as a conqueror", but he also assured the British that he had no desire to destroy the British Empire. If war continued it would, Hitler concluded, be Britain's choice.

A fighting column from the South Wales Borderers in a training exercise in Bootle, Liverpool, 16 August 1940. All over the country soldiers prepared for the threatened German invasion.

In Britain there had been talk since late May in some political circles of reaching a compromise peace, but Churchill was irrevocably committed to fighting on and that became the official position. Hitler's speech was almost disregarded, evoking a brief rebuttal by Lord Halifax, the Foreign Secretary, on 22 July. German leaders found the British position hard to understand, but on 23 July the German press were officially informed by the government that the war would continue. At Hitler's headquarters, Operation "Sealion" now became a serious option, though it soon became clear that there were many barriers to its operational feasibility. The German navy, whose commander-in-chief, Grand Admiral Raeder, had been among the first to suggest invasion to Hitler in June, remained hesitant over recommending a hazardous cross-Channel operation against British air power and the Royal Navy. The destruction of the RAF was a priority without which invasion was regarded as too risky.

The tentative date set for a landing was 15 September. The invasion plan was for six divisions from the 9th and 16th armies to invade on a broad front from Hythe in Kent to Newhaven and Rottingdean on the Sussex coast. The armies would then move rapidly inland, supported by the German air force, to reach a preliminary line running from Gravesend to Portsmouth, and after capturing London to a second line between the Essex coast and the Severn Estuary. Barges and small boats were gathered from all over occupied Europe to ports along the French, Belgian and Dutch coasts and intensive training in beach assault undertaken over the summer. Bomber Command kept up a relentless attack on the invasion ports which added to the many difficulties of organizing a large-scale maritime invasion, something that the German armed forces had done only against light resistance in Norway, and then at great cost in shipping losses. On 30 August, with no clear sign that the Royal Air Force had been defeated, the invasion date was switched to 20 September. In Britain, expectation of invasion marked the whole of September. On 7 September, the codeword "Cromwell" was issued to all units to be on full alert. The weekend of 14–15 September was widely regarded as the most likely date, and as troops moved into position along the coast they were ordered to sleep with their boots on. When nothing happened, the full alert was dropped, to be reinstated on 22 September. Only in late October was the signal "invasion improbable" sent out to units.

On the German side there were mixed feelings about the risk of invasion. Defeat would not have been disastrous but would have been politically unfortunate. At a meeting on 14 September, with British forces at full alert and the RAF undefeated, Hitler announced that although preparations were complete, the invasion of Britain was too risky. He proposed a review two days later for possible landings on 27 September or 8 October, but the situation had not improved. On 19 September, the preparations were ordered to be scaled down and the invasion shipping was dispersed from the vulnerable North Sea ports. On 12 October, Hitler finally ordered "Sealion" to be dismantled. Fear of the Royal Navy and the failure to dent British air power rendered invasion impossible. Hitler ordered a sustained air attack on British cities in case the British government could be terrorized into surrender.

FIELD MARSHAL EDMUND IRONSIDE (1880–1959)

William Edmund Ironside was a soldier of the old school who served in every conflict in which British forces fought from the Boer War onwards, including the ill-fated British intervention in the Russian Civil War at Archangel in 1918–19. Close to retirement by the 1930s, he was chosen at the outbreak of the Second World War to succeed Gort as Chief of the Imperial General Staff, a role in which he tried to pressure the government to begin military action. He misjudged Polish strength in 1939 and German strength in 1940 and was replaced at the height of the Battle of France on 27 May. He was appointed to command the Home Forces for the expected invasion of England but had a poor professional relationship with Churchill and was finally retired for good in the midst of making extensive preparations to reform the home army and to repel the expected invasion.

27 JUNE 1940
German air force proposes landing in England.

16 JULY 1940
Hitler issues "Sealion" directive.

9 AUGUST 1940
British garrison pulled out of Shanghai for use on other fronts.

13 SEPTEMBER 1940
Italian army enters Egypt.

7 OCTOBER 1940
German forces occupy Romania to protect oil interests.

12 OCTOBER 1940
Hitler postpones "Sealion" indefinitely.

THE ROYAL NAVY AT SCAPA FLOW

The Royal Navy's major base in the bleak anchorage at Scapa Flow in the Orkney Islands, off the north Scottish coast, was a permanent threat to any German invasion plans. The base was attacked on 14 October 1939 by a German submarine that managed to evade the defences. The battleship HMS *Royal Oak* was sunk with the loss of 833 lives. After this efforts were made to make the base more secure and the attacks were not repeated. Scapa Flow was out of effective range of German bomber and dive-bomber aircraft, which made it an ideal area to concentrate the main units of the fleet. During the invasion crisis the Royal Navy was prepared for large-scale intervention, a fact that encouraged Admiral Raeder to tell Hitler on 14 September 1940 that the risk was too great to undertake "Sealion".

LEFT Sappers of 211 Field Park Company, Royal Engineers, make "Molotov cocktails" from beer bottles at a base in Yorkshire, to be used for the expected German invasion.

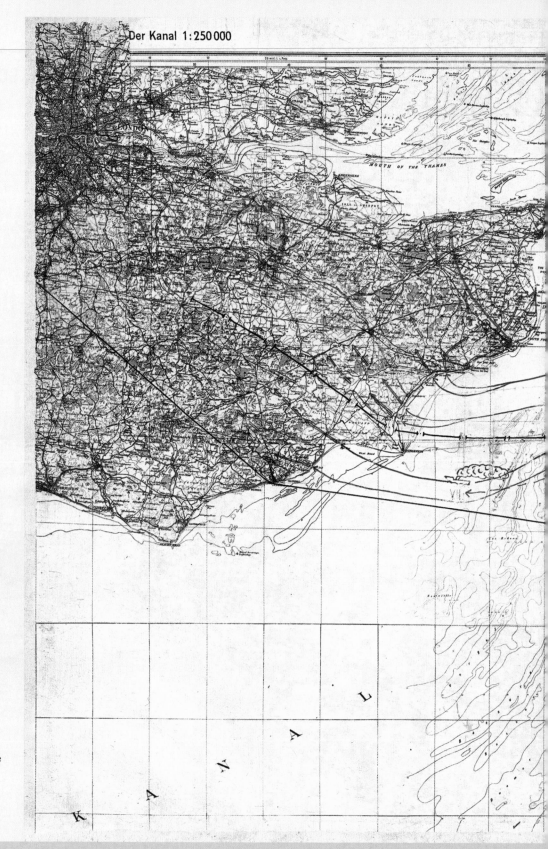

Der Kanal 1:250 000

OPERATION "SEALION" MAP

German operational map of the proposed landings in southern England in September 1940.

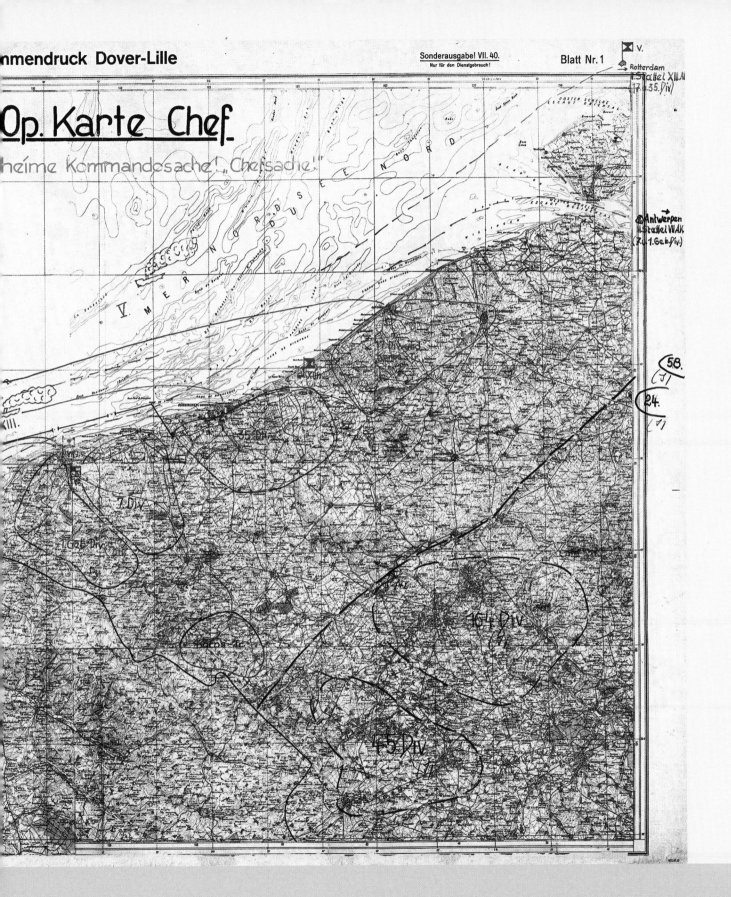

mmendruck Dover-Lille   Sonderausgabe! VII. 40.   Blatt Nr. 1

Nur für den Dienstgebrauch!

Op. Karte Chef

heime Kommandosache! „Chefsache"

7 SEPTEMBER 1940–16 MAY 1941

THE GERMAN BLITZ ON BRITAIN

The heavy bombing of British cities began with an attack on London on 7 September 1940. Bombing had been conducted intermittently against ports and other military and economic installations since June. In July, 258 civilians had been killed; in August 1,075. The first attacks on the London area began on 18–19 August and on central London on the night of 22–23 August. A heavy attack took place on Liverpool on 28–29 August. The attack on 7 September, however, was the first to be carried out in response to Hitler's orders issued on 5 September to destroy the industrial, military and supply systems of the capital. The 350 German bombers who attacked the docks in east London two days later initiated what became known in Britain as "the Blitz".

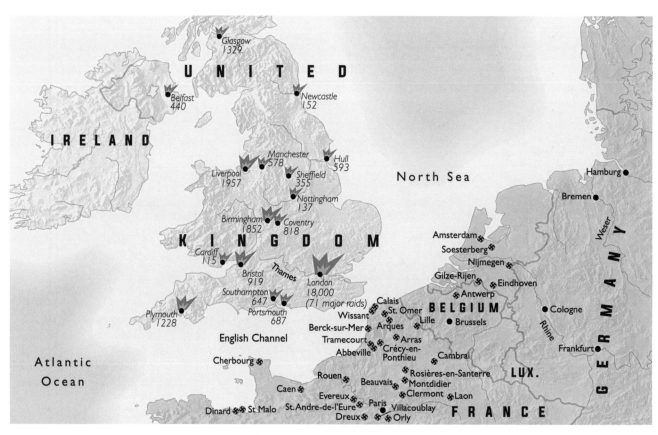

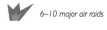 1–5 major air raids	6–10 major air raids	more than 10 major air raids	647 bomb tonnage dropped per city	Luftwaffe bomber base

The German plan was to degrade Britain's capacity to wage war and to undermine the war-willingness of the population, but once the invasion plans were suspended in mid-September, the attacks assumed a more directly political purpose. German leaders hoped that the attacks on cities would force Britain to negotiate and make invasion unnecessary, and on 16 September Göring ordered the new phase of city bombings to begin in earnest. Up to 5 October, there were 35 major air assaults, 18 of them against London, and all conducted in daylight. Unsupportable loss rates forced the German air force to switch to night bombing, and from early October until 16 May 1941, German aircraft attacked a wide range of major cities on nights when the weather conditions permitted. The air units were instructed to attack specific targets and they were helped in this by a system of radio navigation beams known as Knickebein, which worked effectively until British scientists found ways to jam the German beams during November and December 1940. During the campaign German aircraft also used navigation systems known as X-Gerät and Y-Gerät but these too became subject to increasingly effective jamming.

The Blitz was concentrated on London, which was attacked for 57 days in a row between 7 September and 2 November, and then regularly until 10 May. The most famous day of the Blitz was the night of 29 December when a large part of the City of London was destroyed by 136 German bombers. It was on that night that the symbolic photograph was taken of St Paul's Cathedral rising above the flames and smoke. The Blitz was also directed at most British ports and industrial centres, from Belfast in Northern Ireland to Glasgow in Scotland, and to Plymouth (which was heavily bombed between 21 and 23 April 1941), Southampton and Portsmouth in the south. The raid that provoked the widest publicity was that on Coventry on the night of 14–15 November 1940 which killed 554 people. In the major raids on London, 18,800 tons of bombs were dropped; in major attacks against other cities the total was 11,800 tons. The bombing killed 43,000 people and destroyed or damaged one million

22–23 AUGUST 1940
First bombs fall on central London.

28 AUGUST 1940
Liverpool suffers serious attack.

7 SEPTEMBER 1940
First major raid on London.

21 SEPTEMBER 1940
Permission given for Londoners to shelter in the Underground system.

16 NOVEMBER 1940
RAF bombers attack the German city of Hamburg.

29–30 DECEMBER 1940
Bombers destroy large part of the City of London.

6 FEBRUARY 1941
Hitler orders attacks on ports.

20 FEBRUARY 1941
British and German forces clash for the first time in desert war.

10–11 MAY 1941
1,400 killed in final large raid on London.

houses, but did little serious or long-term damage to the British economy or military effort.

The British response focused on both active and passive defence. By May 1941, there were 16 squadrons of night fighters which became more effective as the battle wore on but found it difficult to locate the bombers without sophisticated detection devices. There were 1,785 heavy and light anti-aircraft guns in the summer of 1940, and over 4,500 searchlights, though these too were of limited effectiveness. A high proportion of German losses during the Blitz came from accidents to crews flying long distances in poor weather conditions. The passive defences were organized country-wide by more than two million volunteers of the Air

GENERAL HANS JESCHONNEK
(1899–1943)

Hans Jeschonnek was appointed Chief of the Air Force Staff by Hermann Göring on 1 February 1939 after a meteoric rise through the fledgling German air force. He had joined the German army aged 15 at the outbreak of the First World War and rose to be a lieutenant by 1917, when he joined the air service. He then returned to army duties and joined the German air force in September 1933 when it was still secret. He became Operations Chief in February 1938 and a year later Chief of Staff. He favoured tactical air power in support of the army, but argued for terror attacks against British cities in September 1940 following failure in the Battle of Britain. Struggling to keep the Allied bombers at bay and subject to growing criticism, Jeschonnek finally committed suicide on 18 August 1943 at Hitler's headquarters in East Prussia, after the heavy bombing raid on the rocket research station at Peenemünde.

Raid Precautions organization, including evacuation and the distribution of gas masks. By 1940, around 2.5 million cheap Anderson bomb shelters – named after Sir John Anderson, responsible for Civil Defence measures – had been produced for householders, and in every city deep concrete bunkers were constructed or cellars and underground facilities converted. Nevertheless, civilian casualties were high and in many of the most heavily attacked cities there was an exodus from the threatened area and evidence of demoralization and rising crime levels. The government made many concessions, which included the use of parts of the London Underground network as improvised air-raid shelters, and domestic morale stiffened as the Blitz continued. When it finally ended in May 1941, Britain was more, rather than less, determined to continue to fight.

GENERAL SIR FREDERICK PILE
(1884–1976)

A career artillery officer who rose to the rank of major in the First World War, Frederick Pile was a gifted organizer and a keen modernizer. He played an important part at the War Office between 1928 and 1932 in planning the mechanization of the armed forces. After a brief period in Egypt, he returned in 1937 to command the London 1st Anti-Aircraft Division. On 28 July 1939, he was appointed commander of Anti-Aircraft Command, a post that he filled throughout the war, the only senior commander to do so in the British army. He reorganized Britain's anti-aircraft defences, expanded the supply of guns and shells and, when labour shortages took men away, he recruited 74,000 women into the anti-aircraft ranks. After the war he took up a business career.

LEFT The London Fire Brigade at Eastcheap in the City of London. By the end of 1940 around 20,000 incendiary bombs had been dropped on the capital.

ABOVE General Sir Frederick Pile watches the firing of Britain's "rocket gun" on the South West Coast, 1944.

GERMAN INVASION OF YUGOSLAVIA AND GREECE

The Balkans played very little part in the early stages of the Second World War but the growing interest of the Soviet Union in extending its influence at the expense of Romania and Bulgaria forced Hitler to increase German political authority and military presence in the region. German forces were stationed in Romania from September 1940 to safeguard German supplies of oil from the Ploesti oilfields, while Hungary and Romania joined the Tripartite Pact in November 1940. Strong diplomatic pressure was maintained on Bulgaria and Yugoslavia to retain them in the Axis sphere of influence. At the height of this initiative, Mussolini decided to present his fellow dictator with an Italian triumph by invading Greece. He told none of his Axis partners of his intention and the attack was completely unprovoked. On 28 October, Italian forces attacked across the Albanian-Greek frontier, pitching six Italian against four Greek divisions. The Greek army resisted and with British air support drove back the Italian forces 80km (50 miles) into Albania in December 1940. By early January, most of southern Albania was in Greek hands.

For Hitler, preparing to invade the Soviet Union in late spring the next year, the Italian crisis was an unwelcome diversion. On 4 November 1940, he ordered the armed forces to prepare Operation "Marita", a German invasion of Greece. Bulgaria agreed to allow the passage of German troops, while pressure on Yugoslavia eventually produced agreement on 25 March 1941 to join the Tripartite Pact. In Greece, an accord was reached on 23 February for a British Empire expeditionary force to help the Greeks resist the Italians. W Force, composed mainly of British Empire forces from Australia and New Zealand, arrived in Greece on 7 March, though British forces had been based on the islands of Crete and Lemnos since October 1940. A fresh Italian offensive on 9 March with 28 divisions was again halted with British assistance. Secret ULTRA decrypts of German messages sent using the Enigma machine alerted the British to the new threat from Germany, but the Greeks failed to pull back their forces on the northern frontier with Bulgaria to a better defensive position, as the British commanders wanted. Just as German forces moved forward to begin the assault on Greece, a coup in Belgrade resulted in the new Yugoslav government repudiating the Tripartite agreement with Germany. Hitler ordered an extended campaign against both Yugoslavia and Greece, and on 6 April launched a devastating air attack on Belgrade,

GENERAL IOANNIS METAXAS
(1871–1941)

In April 1936, General Metaxas was chosen as prime minister by the Greek king, George II, who had returned only recently from exile after a long period of republican rule. Metaxas was a successful staff officer from the First World War who turned to politics in the 1920s, leading a small Greek nationalist party which was hostile to parliamentary rule. When a general strike was threatened in the late summer of 1936, Metaxas declared martial law, suspended parliament and inaugurated a dictatorship of the "Third Hellenic Civilization" on 4 August. Despite his imitation of aspects of fascism, he was determined to retain Greek neutrality after the outbreak of war and was sympathetic to the British cause. When Mussolini presented an ultimatum on 28 October 1940, Metaxas rejected it. After the war the date was declared a national holiday as Okhi ("No") Day. Metaxas died in January 1941 but lived long enough to see Greek forces humiliate the Italian army.

28 OCTOBER 1940
Italy invades Greece on pretext
of Greek aggression.

29 JANUARY 1941
Greek prime minister Metaxas dies.

27 MARCH 1941
Hitler decides on invasion
of Yugoslavia.

10 APRIL 1941
Rommel begins siege of Allied
forces in Tobruk.

13 APRIL 1941
Soviet-Japanese Non Agression
Pact signed.

17 APRIL 1941
Yugoslav surrender signed
in Belgrade.

23 APRIL 1941
Greek king and government
evacuate to Crete.

killing 17,000 people, while Field Marshal List's 12th Army assaulted
Greece and southern Yugoslavia.

The Yugoslav campaign was improvised in a remarkably short time, but
its impact was overwhelming. On 8 and 10 April, German, Hungarian and
Italian armies attacked northern and central Yugoslavia, reaching Belgrade
by 12 April. On 18 April, Yugoslavia capitulated following the mutiny of

ABOVE Hitler welcomes the Yugoslav prime minister, Zwetkowitsch, to Berchtesgaden
for talks in February 1941. The German leader hoped to get support from Yugoslavia for
German military action in the Balkans and the Yugoslav signature of the Tripartite Pact.

LEFT Badge of the Greek Sacred Squadron, part of the SAS, formed in 1942 to carry out raids on German occupied Greece.

RIGHT German troops advance into a Serbian village in April 1941 during the rapid conquest of the country. Serbian partisans later organized major resistance from the mountain strongholds of the country.

the Croatian units, its army of over one million men having inflicted just 151 dead on the German forces. The rapid defeat of Yugoslavia doomed Greece, as German forces poured down from southern Yugoslavia and across the "Metaxas" line on the Greek-Bulgarian border. Despite stiff resistance, the Greek and British Empire forces became divided. Although the RAF sent substantial forces to Greece, they were overwhelmed by the German air force, losing 209 aircraft from the Middle East Command's limited reserves. On 23 April, General Tsolakoglou signed the Greek surrender, while 50,000 British Empire and Greek troops were evacuated from the south coast of Greece by a Royal Navy force, some to the island of Crete, some to Egypt. This was the second time in less than a year that British forces had been compelled to abandon mainland Europe by the German army. For Hitler, the diversion had secured his right flank for the invasion of the Soviet Union, protected Romanian oil supplies and inflicted a humiliation on both his Italian ally and his British enemy.

FIELD MARSHAL WILHELM LIST
(1880–1971)

Wilhelm List was one of the most successful of the commanders in Hitler's new German army. He commanded German troops in Austria after the Anschluss and was appointed a general in April 1939. He led the German 14th Army during the Polish campaign and the 12th army in the invasion of France, and was promoted field marshal in July 1940 as a reward. His 12th Army successfully seized Yugoslavia and Greece in April 1941, and he became Commander-in-Chief South East until October 1941. During this period he approved an order

for killing 100 hostages for every German soldier killed. He was transferred to the Eastern Front, where he commanded the assault on the Caucasus in summer 1942. His failure there led to his dismissal in September 1942 and he retired from military life. He was tried as a war criminal in 1948 for atrocities committed in the Balkans under his command, but served only four years of a life sentence.

SINKING THE *BISMARCK*

All the evidence from the first 18 months of the war showed that the traditional role of naval vessels had been subverted by the arrival of air power. The German plan to build a fleet to rival the Royal Navy was scrapped on the outbreak of the war. Work continued on only a handful of big ships, which had already been laid down. The most up-to-date and largest German battleship was the 41,000-ton *Bismarck*, launched on 14 February 1939 and commissioned on 24 August 1940. The ship was intended as a convoy raider in the Atlantic, and her design reflected this, with a broad beam to cope with heavy seas and large fuel tanks. The break-out into the Atlantic, codenamed Operation "Rhine Exercise", was planned to include the battlecruisers *Gneisenau* and *Scharnhorst* and the new battleship *Tirpitz*, but the first two were damaged or under repair and the *Tirpitz* was still engaged in trials before full commissioning. The original force would have been a formidable fleet, but in the end *Bismarck* left on 18 May 1941 accompanied only by the heavy cruiser *Prinz Eugen*.

The commander of the operation, Vice Admiral Lütjens, had reservations about its feasibility but he obeyed commands to the letter, anxious not to be sacked like his predecessor, Vice Admiral Wilhelm Marschall, for disobeying orders. The British were forewarned of the break-out through ULTRA intelligence and from Swedish and Norwegian sources. The ship was spotted by a Spitfire reconnaissance aircraft near Bergen, but contact was not made until 23 May, when the German units entered the Denmark Strait between Iceland and Greenland and a radar-equipped heavy cruiser, HMS *Norfolk*, detected them. The force was shadowed until heavier British ships became available. Early in the morning of 24 May 1941, the new British battleship *Prince of Wales* arrived, accompanied by the battlecruiser *Hood* commanded by Vice Admiral Lancelot Holland. Within minutes, *Hood* had been hit by accurate German gunfire, and at 6.00 a.m. blew up and then sank in three minutes with the loss of all but three of the 1,418 crew. Captain Lindemann aboard *Bismarck* wanted to pursue and destroy the *Prince of Wales*, which had also sustained serious damage, but Lütjens obeyed his instructions not to engage heavy enemy units and insisted on moving on. *Bismarck* had also been damaged: the forward radar was not operational and the fuel tanks were leaking, forcing her to reduce speed to 20 knots. *Prinz Eugen* made off into the Atlantic while *Bismarck* made for the French coast at St Nazaire for essential repairs.

The British shadowed the battleship, but a sudden turn by *Bismarck* confused the pursuers and contact was lost. Only Lütjens's insistence – against Lindemann's advice – on sending a half-hour radio message, which was duly intercepted by the British, gave a clue to the ship's whereabouts, but the pursuing battleship *King George V* miscalculated the position and the German ship drew closer to air cover and destroyer assistance from France. But on 26 May, a Catalina flying-boat of Coastal Command spotted

Bismarck and at 9.00 p.m. that evening a Swordfish torpedo-bomber from the carrier *Ark Royal* succeeded in scoring a hit that jammed the rudder and steering equipment. On the morning of 27 May, the British battleships *Rodney* and *King George V* moved in for the kill, bombarding a slow and listing target and, just after 9.00 a.m., destroying the bridge and eliminating the ship's command. The final sinking is usually attributed to the torpedoes of the destroyer HMS *Dorsetshire* which fired three at the *Bismarck* shortly before the ship sank, at 10.39 a.m., with the loss of all but 100 of more than 2,000 crewmen. Recent research of the wreckage and the testimony of survivors have suggested that the German battleship was scuttled rather than sunk by the enemy. The end of *Bismarck* epitomized Grand Admiral Raeder's gloomy hope, expressed when war broke out, that his men would understand "how to die gallantly" in what he always viewed as an unequal struggle with the Royal Navy. In reality, it was one aircraft that succeeded in slowing down and disabling *Bismarck*, further testimony that the days of traditional fleet engagements were now in the past.

15 APRIL 1940
British intelligence cracks part of the Enigma Code.

10–11 MAY 1941
London hit by heaviest air raid of the war leaving 1,500 dead.

15 MAY 1941
US takes over Vichy French ships in American ports.

18 MAY 1941
Bismarck and *Prinz Eugen* sail for the Atlantic.

27 MAY 1941
Bismarck sunk by Royal Naval destroyers.

HITLER'S MESSAGE

An intercepted message from
Adolf Hitler to the crew of
the *Bismarck* encouraging their
continued resistance.

122

```
TO I D 8 G                        ZTP/1054
FROM GERMAN NAVAL SECTION G C AND C S

110/4595 KC/S                          TOI 0025/27/5/41
                  TOO 0153
TO  FLEET W 70
ENEMY REPORT:
TO C IN C AFLOAT:
I THANK YOU IN THE NAME OF THE ENTIRE GERMAN PEOPLE.  ADOLF
HITLER
TO THE CREW OF THE BATTLESHIP BISMARCK:
ALL GERMANY IS WITH YOU.  ALL THAT CAN STILL BE DONE, WILL BE
DONE.  YOUR DEVOTION TO DUTY WILL FORTIFY OUR PEOPLE IN THEIR
STRUGGLE FOR EXISTENCE.  ADOLF HITLER.

TOO 2229/29/5/41+++AGT+/++
```

BELOW The *Bismarck* on fire on
27 May 1941, photographed from one
of the Royal Navy vessels shadowing
her last hours.

HITLER TURNS EAST

Hitler had since the 1920s thought that a natural area for German imperial expansion lay in the agriculturally and raw-material rich territories of the western Soviet Union. This was the area designated as "living space" (*Lebensraum*) for the German master race. "Russia," Hitler once remarked, "will be our India." He also displayed a visceral hatred of "Jewish Bolshevism", which he thought menaced European civilization and threatened the degeneration of the German race. These ideas formed the background of his decision to settle accounts with the Soviet Union once and for all, an ambition laid down in War Directive 21 for Operation "Barbarossa" signed on 18 December 1940.

The more immediate roots of the German-Soviet conflict lay in Hitler's view of the international situation in 1940. Unable to defeat the British Empire and anxious about the nascent threat of the United States, on 31 July 1940 Hitler called his military leaders together and announced that he wanted to launch an annihilating attack on the Soviet Union the following spring "to smash the state heavily in one blow". Such a move would remove Britain's last potential ally, Hitler argued, and make it impossible for the United States to intervene in Europe. Planning was undertaken over the autumn months, led by the same General Paulus who later surrendered at Stalingrad.

The Soviet Union had taken advantage of Hitler's war in the west to extend its influence in eastern Europe, first occupying the Baltic States in June 1940, then compelling Romania to hand over the territory of Bessarabia and northern Bukovina. In November 1940, Molotov was invited to Berlin to try to gauge the extent of Soviet ambitions. Molotov's desire for Soviet bases in Bulgaria and Turkey confirmed Hitler's view that the Soviet Union posed an immediate strategic and military threat, and he ordered active preparations for invasion to begin. On 5 December, he approved the military plans for a massive three-pronged invasion of the whole Soviet western frontier and timetabled the attack for May 1941. Hitler thought German forces were well prepared – "visibly at their zenith" – while the Red Army was at "an unmistakable nadir". All the military planners assumed the war could be won in a matter of weeks.

The Soviet leadership was divided on the threat posed by Germany, but because Stalin insisted, right up to the day of invasion, that Hitler was too involved in the war in the west to risk a two-front conflict, inadequate preparations were made to meet the German onslaught. A new set of frontier defences, the Stalin Line, built along the new frontier in Poland and the Baltic States, was unfinished by 1941. Soviet strategic planning was based on the idea that if an enemy did attack, light frontier forces would hold the invaders

up for several weeks while the bulk of the Red Army mobilized in the rear and then prepared for a hammer-blow to drive the enemy back on to his own territory. Little account was taken of the lessons of 1939 and 1940 about the power of fast mobile armoured divisions supported strongly by aircraft.

Stalin did think that Germany might risk war at a later date, but wanted time to complete defensive preparations and modernize Soviet forces. Despite strict instructions from Hitler to keep all preparations secret and to pretend that the invasion of Britain was still a priority, the Soviet leadership was given regular intelligence warnings of German intentions in the months leading up to invasion, including the original plan to invade in May and the modified decision to postpone until 22 June. Stalin dismissed it as attempts at provocation by the British to get the Soviet Union to do their fighting for them. Only in May did the new army chief of staff, General Georgii Zhukov, order a stealthy mobilization, but out of 33 divisions planned for redeployment to the western areas, only four or five were ready by the time of invasion. Only on 19 June did the order go out to begin camouflaging airfields and most were unconcealed by the time German aircraft attacked.

During the preparations for "Barbarossa" Hitler succeeded in recruiting Finland, Hungary, Romania and Slovakia as co-belligerents in the campaign. The initial date for a May attack was changed to 22 June to allow for final preparations after the intervention in the Balkans. On the eve of the "Barbarossa" campaign, there were 153 Axis divisions, including an estimated 3.3 million Germans and 650,000 allied troops, the largest invasion force ever assembled. Opposed were 186 Soviet divisions with three million men. On paper Soviet aircraft and tanks outnumbered the Axis – 11,000 tanks against 4,000, and 9,100 aircraft against 4,400 – but they were parcelled out among all the army units and were poorly organized to oppose a concentrated assault. When Axis forces in the early morning of 22 June smashed across the Soviet frontier, surprise was almost complete and the effect devastating.

9 DECEMBER 1940
First British offensive in the Western Desert begins.

29 DECEMBER 1940
Roosevelt pledges that the US will be "the great arsenal of democracy".

30 JANUARY 1941
Germany threatens to attack all neutral shipping supplying Britain.

27 MARCH 1941
Coup in Belgrade – Yugoslavia – renounces the Tripartite Pact.

10 MAY 1941
Rudolf Hess, Hitler's deputy, flies to Britain to broker peace.

27 MAY 1941
Roosevelt declares unlimited national emergency.

14 JUNE 1941
German and Italian assets frozen in the US.

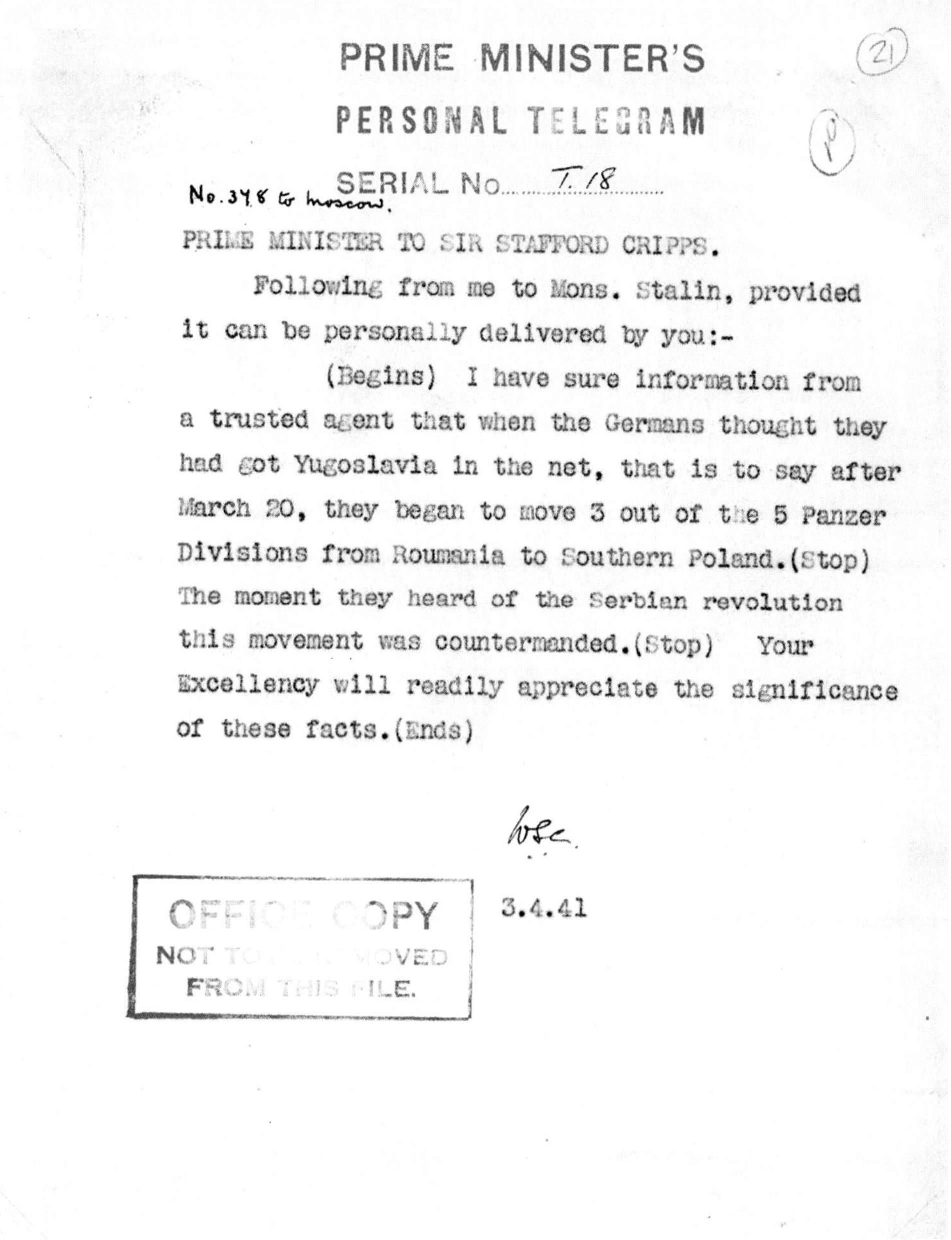

PRIME MINISTER'S

PERSONAL TELEGRAM

(21)

No. 348 to Moscow. SERIAL No. T. 18

PRIME MINISTER TO SIR STAFFORD CRIPPS.

Following from me to Mons. Stalin, provided it can be personally delivered by you:-

(Begins) I have sure information from a trusted agent that when the Germans thought they had got Yugoslavia in the net, that is to say after March 20, they began to move 3 out of the 5 Panzer Divisions from Roumania to Southern Poland.(Stop) The moment they heard of the Serbian revolution this movement was countermanded.(Stop) Your Excellency will readily appreciate the significance of these facts.(Ends)

OFFICE COPY NOT TO BE REMOVED FROM THIS FILE.

3.4.41

CHURCHILL'S TELEGRAM TO STALIN

Telegram from Winston Churchill to the British ambassador in Moscow asking him to pass on a warning to Stalin that the Germans might be intending to attack the Soviet Union. He was cautious in the wording for fear of betraying that the British could read German enigma signals.

OPERATION "BARBAROSSA"

The attack by Axis armies on 22 June 1941 along the whole length of the Soviet western frontier was an overwhelming success. The Soviet plan to hold the attack at the frontier was torn apart in hours and the Red Army was given no time to mobilize a large force to push the enemy back across the frontier, as Soviet military doctrine dictated. The Soviet forces fought with often suicidal determination but from the outset the German plan completely unhinged Soviet military preparations and exposed the Red Army to a looming catastrophe.

The German forces were organized in three main army groups – North, Centre and South. Each attacked on a different axis, using four armoured (Panzer) groups to force a way through the Soviet line while the vast infantry armies followed behind at their own pace. In the far north, Finnish armies supported the assault; in the south large Romanian forces, directed by a German overall commander, moved towards Odessa and the Crimea. The armour ploughed forward at a rapid pace, sometimes covering 30 kilometres (19 miles) a day. By the

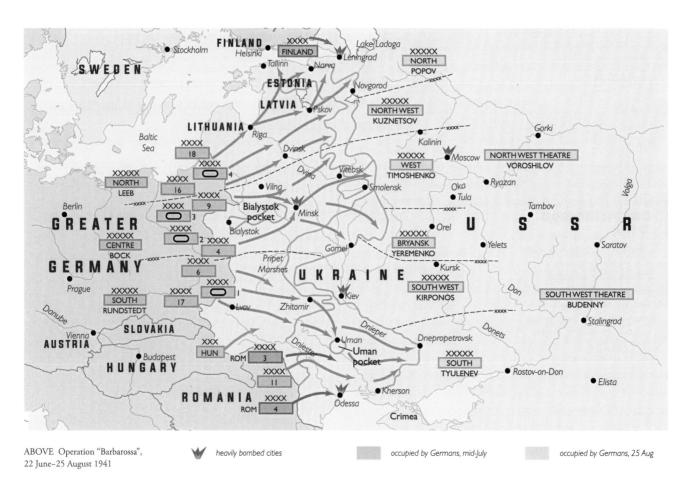

ABOVE Operation "Barbarossa", 22 June–25 August 1941

W heavily bombed cities

occupied by Germans, mid-July

occupied by Germans, 25 Aug

The bodies of Soviet soldiers killed in the determined defence of the frontier fortress at Brest-Litovsk in June and July 1941. The 3,500 men of the garrison fought almost literally to the last man, long after German forces had moved on hundreds of miles into the Soviet Union.

end of June, Army Group North was across Lithuania and deep into Latvia, whose capital fell on 1 July. By 19 August, General Hoeppner's 4th Panzer Group had reached the outskirts of Leningrad and a few weeks later the city was surrounded and under siege. Progress was slower in the south, but by 5 August Odessa too was under siege by Romanian armies, and finally captured in mid-October.

The most spectacular advances were made by Army Group Centre under Field Marshal von Bock. By 28 June, 2nd and 3rd Panzer Groups had encircled the Belorussian capital, Minsk, and trapped 280,000 Soviet soldiers. The fast-moving German armour cut two pincers through the Soviet front and then closed them, forming one pocket after another. Although Soviet forces fought bravely and held up the German advance in small local battles, the speed and destructiveness of the German attack, which had almost destroyed Soviet air power in a matter of days, led to widespread demoralization and the collapse of Soviet communications and supply. By the autumn, around 90 per cent of existing tank strength had been destroyed, and Soviet losses of manpower approached five million killed, wounded or captured. The sheer scale and brutality of the conflict also took a heavy toll on the attackers. By the end of September,

FIELD MARSHAL FEDOR VON BOCK
(1880–1945)

Descended from a famous Prussian military family, von Bock was a battalion commander in the First World War and rose rapidly in the inter-war years to achieve the rank of general in March 1938, a few days before he commanded the forces that occupied Austria. He led Army Group North in the Polish campaign, and Army Group B in the Battle of France. For the invasion of the Soviet Union, he was given command of Army Group Centre, which came within a few kilometres of the centre of Moscow in December 1941. He then commanded Army Group South for the invasion of southern Russia in 1942, but after failing to do what Hitler wanted was replaced in July and never served in command again. He was almost a caricature of a Prussian general, stiff, hard-working and arrogant, though he was no supporter of National Socialism. He was killed in his car by a British aircraft on 4 May 1945.

MARSHAL SEMYON TIMOSHENKO
(1895–1970)

An NCO in the Tsarist cavalry, Timoshenko became a commander in the First Cavalry Army under Stalin's leadership during the Russian Civil War. The Red Army purges led to his rapid promotion, and by 1939 he was commander of the Ukrainian Front Army that occupied eastern Poland. He was appointed to command armies in the Finnish war after the early disastrous Soviet defeats and in March 1940 forced an armistice on the Finns. In May 1940, he became a Marshal of the Soviet Union and Commissar for Defence. When the Germans invaded he was sent to organize the western front and held the Germans around Smolensk. Although regarded as one of the best Soviet commanders, he failed in the spring offensive of 1942 against Kharkov and was not given a major command again until August 1944, when he led the First, Second and Third Ukrainian army groups in the long march to Budapest and Vienna. Stalin favoured the officers who had fought with him in the First Cavalry Army and Timoshenko survived his mistakes when other officers did not.

Soviet soldiers wait to be evacuated from the port of Odessa by the Soviet Black Sea Fleet in early October 1941. Around 80,000 troops and 15,000 civilians were rescued before Romanian forces captured the city.

27 JUNE 1941

Hungary declares war on the Soviet Union.

12 JULY 1941

Anglo-Soviet mutual aid treaty signed in Moscow.

27 JULY 1941

Japanese troops begin occupation of Indo-China.

14 AUGUST 1941

Atlantic Charter signed at Placentia Bay, Newfoundland.

25 AUGUST 1941

Joint Anglo-Soviet occupation of Iran.

18 OCTOBER 1941

General Tojo becomes Japanese premier.

around 550,000 German casualties were reported, dwarfing anything the German army had so far experienced.

Despite heavy losses and fierce Soviet resistance, Hitler remained confident that the Soviet Union could be broken. In early September, a Soviet counter-attack at Smolensk was finally beaten off by Army Group Centre, exposing Moscow to the German army. Hitler instead insisted that von Bock's forces support the attack on Leningrad and help the embattled Army Group South against General Kirponos's South West Front. The siege of Leningrad was completed and in the south a spectacular victory was achieved when 1st and 2nd Panzer groups encircled the Ukrainian capital, Kiev, on 15 September and with it 650,000 Soviet soldiers. Around 150,000 others managed to fight their way out but the defeat opened the way to German conquest of the rest of the rich industrial region to the south. On 6 September 1941, Hitler's War Directive 35 finally gave Army Group Centre the opportunity to advance on Moscow.

On the Soviet side the Axis campaign seemed unstoppable. New divisions were mobilized and sent to the front and as quickly disappeared. Stalin made himself Supreme Commander of the Armed Forces on 10 July and Commissar for Defence on 19 July. He ordered harsh treatment for anyone who did not fight to the death. In August, Order 270 was published which condemned any soldier who surrendered as a traitor to the motherland. Senior soldiers were arrested and shot for failing to halt the German onslaught. Timoshenko and Zhukov succeeded in holding up the German advance at Smolensk, and on 6 September the city of Yelna was briefly recaptured from German forces, but the collapse of Soviet resistance was impossible to disguise. By the end of September, most of the huge forces that had opposed the attack were destroyed or captured. Eyewitnesses recall a sense of euphoria at Hitler's headquarters.

RIGHT A woman in Odessa, the Ukrainian port captured by the Romanian army on 16 October 1941. Following its capture an estimated 50,000 Jews were murdered.

8 JUNE–14 JULY 1941

THE ALLIED INVASION OF IRAQ AND SYRIA

With German forces in the Balkans and pressing forward in the Western Desert, British leaders became anxious that the position of British interests in the Middle East, particularly oil, which was vital for the whole war effort in the Mediterranean, might be threatened by a combination of Axis military success and pro-Axis sympathy among the Muslim populations of the Middle East. Plans were discussed as early as March 1940 for possible action in Iraq, where anti-British nationalism was a threat to the Mosul oilfields; Operation "Sabine" was prepared for the possible transfer of troops from India to Basra. When Iraq's regency was overthrown by a military coup in early April 1941, the British ambassador, Sir Kinahan Cornwallis, who arrived in Baghdad in the midst of the coup, urgently requested British military intervention before the anticipated arrival of German aircraft and troops.

Following the defeat of the Iraqi army, which surrendered on 30 May 1941, British forces occupied Baghdad. They can be seen here gazing at the city across the Tigris River.

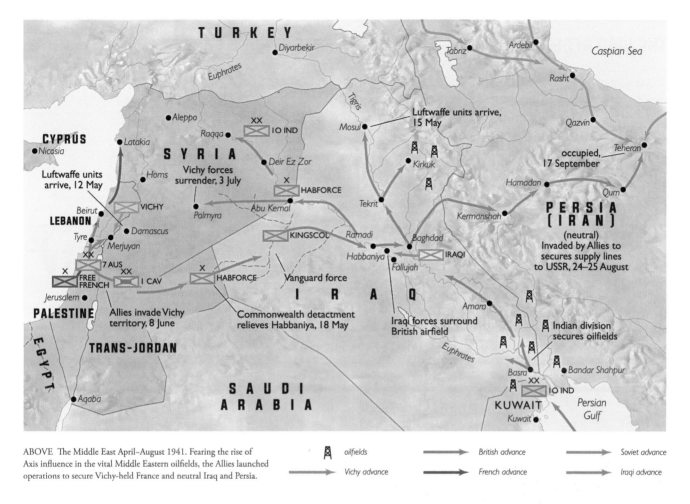

ABOVE The Middle East April–August 1941. Fearing the rise of Axis influence in the vital Middle Eastern oilfields, the Allies launched operations to secure Vichy-held France and neutral Iraq and Persia.

oilfields	British advance
Vichy advance	French advance
	Soviet advance
	Iraqi advance

On 17 April the first Indian troops arrived in Basra and two days later 400 men of the 1st King's Own Royal Regiment flew in to reinforce the Habbaniya air base near Baghdad. The rebel leader, Rashid Ali, decided to destroy the British military presence and on 1 May the Iraqi army began to dig in around the air base to prepare to capture it, hoping that their action would bring German support. The British commander of the base, Air Vice-Marshal Smart, decided to fight and on 2 May, before Iraqi forces were ready, launched a heavy air attack against them. The Iraqi air force of 56 largely obsolete aircraft was soon halved in strength and relentless bombing forced retreat from the perimeter of the base. A relief force was organized from Trans Jordan codenamed "Habforce", under the command of Major General John Clark. Out of almost 6,000 troops, a rapid-movement column of 2,000 was created to reach the air base quickly. By this time around 25 German aircraft were available from Iraqi and Syrian airfields to help the rebels. The advance column was attacked by German bombers, but reached Habbaniya on 18 May.

By this time Iraqi resistance was crumbling. The forces available at the air base moved out to Fallujah on 19 May, captured the town and

2 MAY 1941

British troops occupy Basra and the oilfields of southern Iraq.

10 MAY 1941

London experiences the heaviest air raid of the Blitz.

20 MAY 1941

German paratroops begin the invasion of the island of Crete.

3 JUNE 1941

Anti-Jewish rioters in Baghdad murder Jews and destroy Jewish shops.

11 JUNE 1941

Roosevelt agrees to station US troops in Iceland to replace a British garrison.

12 JULY 1941

Britain and the Soviet Union sign a mutual aid treaty in Moscow.

moved on Baghdad. German air forces were outnumbered and 21 aircraft destroyed. On 30 May, Iraq's five-division army abandoned the fight and an armistice was signed. The Regent returned to power in October and on 17 January 1943 Iraq declared war on the Axis. The help given to Rashid

THE IRAQ REBELLION

Iraq had been a British mandate under the League of Nations but was granted independence in 1932. The Anglo-Iraqi Treaty of 1930 gave the British economic and military concessions, including the right to station troops and two permanent air bases at Basra and Habbaniya. A group of anti-British army officers in Iraq known as the Golden Square, led by the military commander and former prime minister Rashid Ali al-Gaylani (1892–1965), launched a coup against the pro-British Regent Emir Abdullah in early April 1941. Rashid Ali became prime minister again on 3 April and the Regent retreated to Basra. Following the defeat of the Iraqi army in May 1941, Rashid fled to Iran and finally to Germany, where he remained in exile until 1958.

FREE FRENCH FORCES

Free French forces, under the overall command of Charles de Gaulle but operationally subordinate to British officers, played a part in the Middle East campaigns but their presence produced problems for British plans for the region. De Gaulle wanted Syria and Lebanon to be administered by the Free French and to be able to recruit soldiers from the Vichy garrison for the Free French cause. De Gaulle lost the first argument, and had to agree to the principle of Syrian and Lebanese independence, but he won the second, and 6,000 new recruits joined his forces.

Ali from bases in Syria, a French mandate loyal to Vichy France, prompted Churchill to authorize a further operation to secure the Middle East for the Allies. On 23 June, an operation under the command of Lieutenant General Maitland Wilson was launched against the Vichy French in Lebanon and Syria from Palestine in the south and Iraq in the east, using "Habforce" and the 10th Indian Division, which had been landed at Basra during May, as well as the Australian 7th Division. Slow progress was made against the French garrisons, but by 6 July the 7th Australian Division began the battle for Beirut, which followed the occupation of Damascus on 21 June. The commander of Beirut capitulated on 10 July and the Vichy authorities signed an armistice (the Acre Convention) on 14 July. Some 32,300 French troops were repatriated and Syria was placed under British military control until its independence in 1946. Wilson remained in the area, commanding what was now called Ninth Army against the risk of a German thrust from the north through the Soviet Caucasus. The two campaigns secured a vital area that combined Britain's war effort in Europe and Asia and frustrated further Axis advance.

ABOVE Armed tribal warriors gather in an Iraqi village in May 1941 as part of the revolt against the presence of British bases in the country.

RIGHT A Free French fighter from the French colony of Chad mans a machine gun in a city street during the Allied advance into Syria and Lebanon, June 1941.

OPPOSITE British soldiers on 12 July 1941 comb the ruins of the Temple of Bel, near Palmyra in Syria, for Arab snipers employed by the Vichy French regime to obstruct the British advance.

7 DECEMBER 1941

PEARL HARBOR

In the early morning of 7 December (8 December in Japan), waves of Japanese naval aircraft with bombs and torpedoes attacked the major United States naval base at Pearl Harbor on Oahu in the Hawaiian Islands. They attacked without warning or a declaration of war and unleashed four years of conflict in the Pacific, which would end with the final destruction of the Japanese Empire.

A naval launch approaches the US battleship *West Virginia*, hit by six torpedoes during the attack by Japanese aircraft on the base at Pearl Harbor. Altogether 2,403 civilians and servicemen were killed in the attacks.

The assault on Pearl Harbor came at the end of a long deterioration in relations between Japan and the United States. The American government favoured the Chinese side in the Sino-Japanese war, but would do nothing to provoke war with Japan. The United States assumed that Japan would never risk all-out war and hoped to arrive eventually at a diplomatic solution. In July 1940, when the first Japanese forces were allowed to enter northern Indo-China, Roosevelt authorized restrictions of scrap steel and oil exports to Japan. Japanese naval planners, anxious about the threat of a total oil embargo, began to argue in favour of a pre-emptive "Southward Advance" against America and the British Empire, seizing the oil-rich region of the Dutch East Indies and establishing an unassailable perimeter in the Pacific.

The German invasion of the Soviet Union created confusion in Japan. The powerful Japanese army argued for the opportunity to settle accounts with Russia by joining forces with Germany in the destruction of the Soviet Union. The navy continued to press for a southern strategy on the grounds that the Soviet-German war reduced any risk in the north, while seizing the rich resources of the south would create conditions for the final triumph against China and the Soviet Union. On 26 July 1941, following further Japanese incursion in Indo-China, the United States froze all Japanese assets and tightened the oil embargo. The navy in early September 1941 proposed a showdown with the United States if diplomatic efforts to reverse American policy were not successful. A deadline was set for 30 November, after which war would be launched. The American government could read Japanese codes and knew that Japanese plans for aggression were hardening. On 26 November, Cordell Hull, Roosevelt's Secretary of State, presented new conditions to Japan for the withdrawal of their forces from Indo-China and China. The Japanese government rejected the idea out of hand, and on 1 December, Emperor Hirohito approved the onset of war.

In early December, a large force made up of all six of Japan's fleet carriers, with 460 aircraft, sailed in complete radio silence for the seas north of Hawaii. Although intelligence did eventually reach the listening station on the islands, it was lost among a mass of detailed radio traffic. An intercepted message to the Japanese Embassy in Washington from Tokyo on 6 December was incompletely decoded so that the instructions to sever diplomatic relations, indicating war, failed to be noticed. At 7.49 a.m. on 7 December the first wave of 177 Japanese bombers, dive-bombers and fighters struck Pearl Harbor and the US air bases. A second wave hit at 8.50 a.m. Of the 394 US aircraft on the island, 347 were destroyed or damaged for the loss of only 29 Japanese planes. Surprise was total and the impact devastating. A corps of highly trained naval pilots succeeded in sinking or damaging 16 warships. Some 76 ships were undamaged, among them the submarines, while US aircraft carriers were by chance not in port. Despite the outrage provoked in the United States at the attack, the damage was not as severe as Japanese planners had hoped and Pearl Harbor remained a central base for subsequent American operations.

10 NOVEMBER 1941

Churchill promises Roosevelt to declare war "within the hour" should Japan attack the United States.

13 NOVEMBER 1941

US Congress repeals parts of the 1939 Neutrality Act to allow the arming of merchant ships.

26 NOVEMBER 1941

Cordell Hull demands the Japanese withdrawal of troops from China.

5 DECEMBER 1941

Hitler halts the German offensive in front of Moscow.

11 DECEMBER 1941

Germany and Italy declare war on the United States.

19 JANUARY 1942

Roosevelt approves funding to develop an atomic bomb.

HIDEKI TOJO
(1884–1948)

General Tojo, the son of a Japanese army general, was appointed Army Minister in 1940 and then prime minister on 16 October 1941. He had little campaign experience, but was a hard-working, strict and effective administrator and military politician. He was a committed nationalist and was at the forefront of those arguing for a tough military policy in China and against compromise with the Western powers. He faced growing criticism in 1944 over Japanese military reverses and was forced to resign in July 1944. He tried and failed to commit suicide when American military police arrived to arrest him in 1945, and was hanged as a war criminal in December 1948.

In Congress the following day Roosevelt condemned "a date which will live in infamy" and war was formally declared against the Japanese Empire. Japanese politicians had hoped that Pearl Harbor would demoralize American opinion and limit their war effort. As it turned out, nothing could have prompted greater outrage and a stronger American urge to fight the war with Japan to the finish.

JAPANESE-AMERICANS

In 1942 around 110,000 Japanese-Americans, many of them American citizens, were "relocated" from their homes, mainly on the West Coast, to ten camps further inland. The move followed President Roosevelt's Executive Order 9066, signed on 19 February 1942, which gave the Secretary of War the right to designate prescribed military areas from which people could be legally and forcibly expelled. Most of the Japanese-Americans were held in the camps for up to three years even though not a single case of spying or sabotage was ever discovered. The same rules were not applied to American citizens of German or Italian descent, but only to German and Italian aliens. Around 22,500 young Japanese-American men volunteered for combat, 18,000 of whom served in segregated units.

A group of Japanese interned in the US-controlled Panama Canal Zone on 10 December 1941. Following the Japanese attack on Hawaii, Japanese, German and Italian citizens in the Zone were forced into an internment camp like those set up throughout the continental United States.

PROPOSED MESSAGE TO THE CONGRESS

Yesterday, December 7, 1941, a date which will live in ~~world history~~ *infamy*, the United States of America was ~~suddenly~~ *suddenly* and deliberately attacked by naval and air forces of the Empire of Japan.

The United States was at the moment at peace with that nation and was *still in* ~~conducting~~ conversations with its Government and its Emperor looking toward the maintenance of peace in the Pacific. Indeed, one hour after Japanese air squadrons had commenced bombing in ~~Hawaii and the Philippines~~ *Oahu* the Japanese Ambassador to the United States and his colleague delivered to the Secretary of State a formal reply to a ~~former~~ *recent American* message. ~~from the Secretary.~~ *While* This reply ~~contained a statement~~ *stated* that diplomatic negotiations *it seemed useless to continue* ~~must be considered at an end, but~~ it contained no threat ~~nor~~ *or* hint of ~~an~~ *war or* armed attack.

It will be recorded that the distance ~~of Hawaii~~ *was* of Hawaii from Japan makes it obvious that the attack ~~was~~ deliberately *or so in weeks* planned many days ago. During the intervening time the Japanese Government has deliberately sought to deceive the United States by false statements and expressions of hope for continued peace.

The attack yesterday on ~~Hawaii and on the island of Oahu have~~ *the Hawaiian Islands has* caused severe damage to American naval and military forces. Very many American lives have been lost. In addition American ~~naval~~ ships have been torpedoed on the high seas between San Francisco and Honolulu.

Yesterday the Japanese Government also launched an attack against Malaya.

Last night Japanese forces attacked Guam.

Japan has, therefore, undertaken a surprise offensive extending *the Philippine Islands* throughout the Pacific area. The facts of yesterday speak for themselves. The people of the United States have already formed their opinions and well understand the implications ~~to the very life~~ *to* very ~~life~~ the safety of our nation.

As Commander-in-Chief of the Army and Navy I have ~~of course~~ directed that all measures be taken for our defense.

Long will we remember the character of the onslaught against us.

(A) *No matter how long it may take us to overcome this premeditated invasion the American people will in their righteous might win through to absolute victory.*

I speak the will of the Congress and of the people ~~of this country~~ when I assert that we will not only defend ourselves to the uttermost but will see to it that this form of treachery shall never endanger us again. Hostilities exist. There is no mincing the fact that our people, our territory and our interests are in grave danger.

I, therefore, ask that the Congress declare that since the unprovoked and dastardly attack by Japan on Sunday, December seventh, a state of war exists *has* between the United States and the Japanese Empire.

****

Our people in

Full confidence in our might

ROOSEVELT'S "DAY OF INFAMY" SPEECH

A draft of President Roosevelt's address to congress following the Japanese attack on Pearl Harbor including Roosevelt's own handwritten amendments. He changed "a date which will live in world history" to "a date which will live in infamy", the phrase that made the speech famous.

8 DECEMBER 1941–11 MAY 1942

BLITZKRIEG IN ASIA

The Japanese attack on Pearl Harbor was planned to coincide with a number of complex and daring combined operations to seize south-east Asia, the East Indies and a string of small islands in the western Pacific to secure supplies of oil, rubber, tin and other minerals, and to discourage the British and American governments from attempting the difficult and expensive task of recapturing the new southern zone of the Japanese Empire. Within four months the vast area of the European powers' empires in the Far East was under Japanese rule.

LEFT Japanese forces were among the first to master effective combined operations. Here Japanese soldiers haul an artillery piece onto the shore from the landing boats during one of many similar operations in the early weeks of 1942.

On 7 December, a Japanese seaborne striking force under General Tomoyuki Yamashita assembled in the Gulf of Siam destined the following day to occupy the Kra Isthmus in southern Thailand and to assault the British airfields in northern Malaya. Other strike forces prepared to seize Hong Kong, assault the Philippines, and then conquer the British and Dutch possessions in the East Indies. The campaign was an extraordinary success. In Malaya Yamashita commanded around 60,000 men, but defeated a British Empire force more than twice as large. The attempt by the Allied army to hold up the Japanese advance was half-hearted at best. By 9 January, the Japanese were almost at the Malayan capital of Kuala Lumpur. Adept at jungle warfare and tactics of infiltration, the Japanese army proved an irresistible force against a poorly prepared enemy with limited air power. By 31 January, Malaya had been abandoned and the British forces were withdrawn to the island of Singapore.

12 DECEMBER 1941
Romania declares war on the United States, followed by Bulgaria the next day.

1 JANUARY 1942
United Nations Declaration signed by Britain, the United States, China and the Soviet Union and 22 other states.

13 JANUARY 1942
German submarines begin Operation "Drumbeat" against shipping along the US Atlantic coastline.

14 FEBRUARY 1942
Directive to RAF Bomber Command allows onset of area bombing of cities.

4 APRIL 1942
Hitler orders retaliatory air raids on British cities.

5 MAY 1942
Allied forces land in northern Madagascar to prevent Japanese occupation.

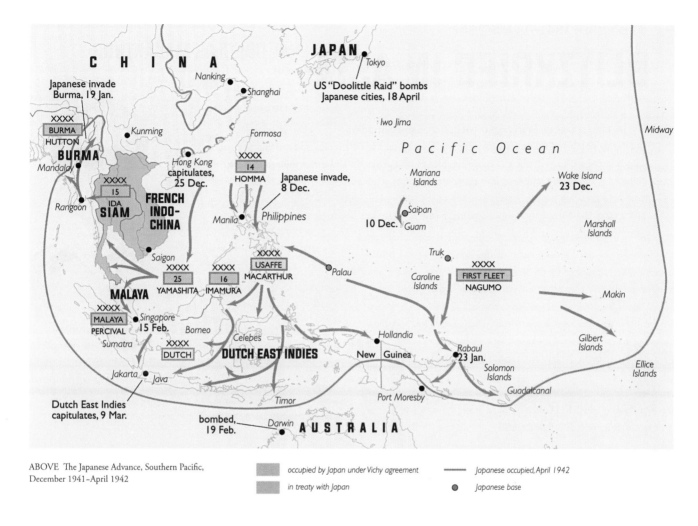

ABOVE The Japanese Advance, Southern Pacific,
December 1941–April 1942

occupied by Japan under Vichy agreement

in treaty with Japan

——— Japanese occupied, April 1942

● Japanese base

Japanese progress in the Philippines was less spectacular. The northernmost island of Batan was occupied on 8 December and the main island of Luzon assaulted by seaborne forces two days later. Further out in the Pacific, small islands were seized to prevent any threat from the central ocean area. The US base at Guam was occupied on 10 December. The garrison on Wake Island resisted the first Japanese attack on 11 December, but succumbed to a larger air and sea assault 12 days later. The attack on the East Indies, defended by Dutch, British, Australian and colonial troops, began a week later on 15 December with landings on the island of Borneo. In a daring series of combined operations the Japanese army

VICE ADMIRAL CHUICHI NAGUMO
(1887–1944)

The leader of the operation at Pearl Harbor, Nagumo was regarded as a particularly aggressive and effective fleet commander, with a reputation for speaking his mind. He rose to prominence in the 1930s as a torpedo expert, and was among the circle of senior Japanese naval officers who favoured a confrontation with the United States. He followed up the Pearl Harbor attack with command of the raids on northern Australia, India and Ceylon (Sri Lanka) and at the Battle of Midway. The disaster at Midway showed the limits of his grasp of naval air power, and he was relieved of command, posted back to Japan and then, in 1944, to the Marianas. He committed suicide in July 1944 during the American invasion of Saipan.

swarmed out over the archipelago, targeting airfields and oil installations. One branch of the assault moved southeast to capture the British Solomon Islands. Admiral Takahashi's task force concentrated on driving through the central zone, taking Bali on 19 February and Timor the next day. The capital of the Dutch East Indies, Batavia (Jakarta), was captured on 5 March. Japanese warships and aircraft hunted down surviving Allied shipping and destroyed it, although some of the Allied force was evacuated to Australia from Java, harried by Japanese aircraft. On 19 February, to drive home the Japanese success, bomber aircraft destroyed a large part of the northern Australian port of Darwin. The Dutch surrendered on 9 March, the rest of the Allies three days later.

Japanese plans worked almost like clockwork. There was no intention of creating a larger campaign area than their limited forces could protect and Australia was safe for the present. In the Indian Ocean the British naval presence, weakened by the sinking of HMS *Prince of Wales* and HMS *Repulse* on 10 December, was challenged by a daring raid led by Vice Admiral Nagumo, whose task force attacked Colombo in Ceylon on 5 April 1942, then the naval base at Trincomalee, sinking four warships, including the carrier *Hermes*, the first to be sunk by carrier aircraft. There was plan yet to extend the Japanese Empire into the Indian Ocean area, but simply the aim to undermine the delicate British political position in southern Asia and to warn Britain to stay at arm's length from the new Japanese Empire, which had been established across thousands of miles in the space of little more than four months.

GENERAL DOUGLAS MACARTHUR
(1880–1964)

MacArthur was born into an upper-class American family, the son of a soldier. He was an outstanding officer cadet, scoring the highest marks ever achieved at the military academy at West Point. At the end of the First World War, he was already a brigadier general. In 1930, he served as Army Chief of Staff, and in 1935 went as military adviser to the Philippines, where he retired from the American army to become a Philippines field marshal. In July 1941, Roosevelt made him commander of US forces in the Far East, and he organized the defence of the Philippines against Japanese assault. He was appointed Commander-in-Chief South West Pacific Area in April 1942, and despite his reputation for flamboyance and self-promotion, became an inspirational leader of men. After recapturing the Philippines in 1945, he was made commander-in-chief of all US army forces in the Pacific. He became Supreme Commander Allied Powers in the post-war administration of Japan and played a key part in Japan's democratic reconstruction. He was finally relieved of command in April 1951 following arguments with President Truman over policy on the Korean War.

On 18 April 1942 US forces launched a reprisal raid on Tokyo and other Japanese cities with 16 B 25 Mitchell bombers launched from the US carrier *Hornet*. The bombers, seen here leaving the carrier, inflicted little physical damage but gave the American public a psychological boost.

THE FALL OF SINGAPORE

The diary of Lieutenant General Arthur Percival. The entries up to 15 February cover the Japanese attack on Singapore; the entries from 26 February were written just over a year later during his time as a POW.

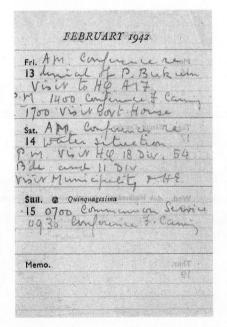

JANUARY—FEBRUARY 1942

Fri. 30 Genl Wavell's visit

Sat. 31 Anti tank defence before blew completed
P.m. Visit 18 Div Area
Issued Order to troops

Sun. 1 FEB. ☉ *Septuagesima*
P.m. Visit A.I.F Sector

Memo.

FEBRUARY 1942

Mon. 2 *Purification*
Candlemas (Scottish Quarter Day)
P.m. Visit 11 Div
Notice in Press

Tues. 3 Lunch 18 Div
A.m. Visit 3 Corps
P.m Visit 54 Bde
and Changi after
air raid

Wed. 4 1000 hrs.
Conference Flagstaff HQ
Press
Civilian to Flagstaff House

Thur. 5 Empress of Asia
sunk
Visit to 44 Bde
front

FEBRUARY 1942

Fri. 6

Sat. 7

Sun. 8 ☾ *Sexagesima*
P.m. Visit HQ A.I.F
Japanese attack
begins

Memo.

FEBRUARY 1942

Mon. 9 1000
Leng Co
1200 visit to HQ A.I.F
1800 Conference Sime Rd

Tues. 10 Genl Wavell's visit
A.m. Visit HQ A.I.F
3 Corps, 11 Div
P.m Visit A.I.F twice

Wed. 11 Moved HQ to F. Canning
Visit A.I.F + B. Timah Rd
HQ 55 Bde

Thur. 12 A.m Visit A.I.F + 55 Bde
+ 3 Corps — then H.E.
P.m. Visit 3 Corps — ordered
withdrawal from Changi

FEBRUARY 1942

Fri. 13 A.m. Conference re
denial of P. Bukum
Visit to HQ A.I.F
P.m 1400 Conference F. Canning
1700 Visit Govt House

Sat. 14 A.m. Conference re
water situation
P.m Visit HQ 18 Div, 54
Bde and 11 Div
Visit Municipality + H.E.

Sun. 15 ☉ *Quinquagesima*
0700 Communion Service
0930 Conference F. Canning

Memo.

FEBRUARY—MARCH 1942

~~**Fri.**~~ **Sat. 27** Much striking of Poros
by sentries etc
Heath knocked about
Submitted letter.

Sat. 28 Much striking by
sentries.

~~**Sun.**~~ **Mon. 1 MARCH** *2nd in Lent   St. David's Day*
Personally hit 4
times by sentry
Report of striking submitted

Memo.

20 JANUARY 1942

THE WANNSEE CONFERENCE

On 20 January 1942, 14 German senior government officials and SS leaders met with Reinhard Heydrich in a villa on the shores of Lake Wannsee in a respectable suburb of Berlin. Heydrich was chief of the Reich Main Security Office (RSHA) responsible for most issues of security and surveillance in the Third Reich and in this role had been formally given the task by Hermann Göring, on 31 July 1941, of implementing a "final solution" to the Jewish question. In mid-July 1941 this meant evacuation of Jews to the newly conquered areas in the east of Europe, but by the time Heydrich met officials at Wannsee the term "evacuation" now signified destruction.

At the 20 January meeting, Heydrich presented figures on the Jewish population in Europe, over 11 million, a total which had been calculated by his assistant, the Gestapo official Adolf Eichmann. Heydrich had been authorized to organize the mass deportation of all Europe's Jews by his immediate superior Heinrich Himmler, head of the elite SS organization. Himmler was almost certainly acting on Hitler's authority, but the exact point at which Hitler ordered the mass murder of the Jews of Europe is not clear. Most historians date the decision to November or early December 1941, but the murder of certain categories of Jews in the conquered areas of the Soviet Union had already begun in June 1941. In August 1941, Hitler approved the murder of Jewish women and children in Russia; in September 1941, the male Jews of Serbia were

3 OCTOBER 1940
Jews in Nazi-occupied Warsaw are ordered into the ghetto.

19 MAY 1941
Hitler issues guidelines for troops in Russia giving permission to murder Communist Jews.

31 JULY 1941
Hermann Göring authorizes Reinhard Heydrich to find a "final solution" to the Jewish question.

18 AUGUST 1941
Hitler orders Berlin's remaining Jews to be deported eastwards.

13 MARCH 1942
The Belzec death camp is opened for the mass murder of Jews.

LEFT The villa on the shores of the Wannsee in Berlin used as an SS guest house during the war. It was here that the notorious Wannsee Conference took place on 20 January 1942 which sealed the fate of Europe's Jews.

OPPOSITE A group of emaciated children in the Warsaw ghetto, January 1942. The Ghetto was sealed up by the German authorities on 16 November 1940 and an estimated 100,000 died of disease and hunger before the population was deported to the death camps.

slaughtered and Jews in the former Polish areas of Warthegau and Galicia were exterminated; and on 15 October 1941 the first mass deportation of German Jews to the east began. The decision to exterminate Jews was thus taken piecemeal across the second half of 1941. The Wannsee Conference was the opportunity for Heydrich to bring all these strands together into a single comprehensive programme of genocide.

To carry out the new policy a number of purpose-built extermination camps were set up on occupied Polish territory at Chelmno, Sobibor, Belzec, Treblinka, Maidanek and Auschwitz-Birkenau. Construction had begun in 1941 of camps that included gas chambers where large numbers of victims could be killed at once using either carbon-monoxide poisoning or – as at Auschwitz – the pesticide Zyklon-B. The first camp with purpose-built gas chambers began operation in March 1942, but before that an estimated 1.4 million Jews had already been killed, most of them in the campaign in the Soviet Union where the Einsatzgruppen, following in the wake of the army, murdered Jews as a potential threat to the German war effort. Himmler was anxious that these so-called "wild killings" made too great a demand on the SS men who did the shootings and favoured the shift to factory-based killing in the extermination camps. From March 1942 until the gassings finished in October 1944,

ADOLF EICHMANN
(1906–62)

From his position as head of the Gestapo office for "Jewish Affairs", Adolf Eichmann played a central role in the task of registering, collecting and deporting the Jewish population of Europe to the death camps in Poland. He was born in Germany but brought up in Austria, where he did a number of salesman's jobs in the 1920s. In 1932 he joined the Austrian National Socialist party and the SS, but a year later moved to Germany and joined the German SS and the security police. He was made responsible for Jewish affairs in Austria after the Anschluss, and in 1939 was promoted to head office IV B 4 (Jewish affairs) in the Reich Main Security Office, which controlled the Gestapo. In this position he oversaw the "final solution of the Jewish question", first organizing emigration and deportation, then supervising the transfer of Jews to the east. In 1950 he fled to Argentina, from where he was snatched by Israeli security agents in May 1960, taken to Israel, put on trial and executed in 1962.

JEWISH RESISTANCE IN THE HOLOCAUST

In Eastern Europe under German occupation thousands of Jews in Poland, Belorussia and Ukraine escaped into the forests and marshlands where they fought as partisans against the occupiers or set up villages and camps where Jews fleeing from the ghettos could be protected. Jewish partisans faced hostility from Ukrainian nationalists and Russian partisan groups, where anti-Semitism remained a strong prejudice. Life for Jewish partisans was harsh. Babies born to women partisans had to be abandoned or killed in case their cries alerted the enemy. Capture meant certain death, and wounded companions were often shot by their own side.

an estimated 3.7 million Jews were murdered in the camps, most of them from Poland, the Baltic states and Czechoslovakia.

The genocide of the European Jews was organized from Berlin on directives from the German leadership but the programme was carried out with the help of many non-German perpetrators. In Romania there was a long tradition of anti-Semitism and the war against the Soviet Union was used as an excuse to deport or murder large numbers of Romanian Jews. In southern Ukraine, the invading Romanian Army perpetrated its own genocide of the Jewish populations in its path. In the Baltic states and Ukraine, the German invaders found enthusiastic local militia and police willing to hunt out or murder Jews. Elsewhere in occupied Europe, local collaborators or fascists helped German officials to identify, assemble and deport Jewish populations. Only in Denmark were almost all Jews saved, by shipping them secretly to Sweden. The Hungarian regime resisted demands for deportation until 1944, when German forces occupied the country. Half of Hungary's Jews perished in Auschwitz-Birkenau in the final months of killing in 1944. The genocide was both a German and a European crime.

ABOVE A group of Jewish partisans pose for the camera sometime in 1942 or 1943 in the Naliboki forest, near Novogrudok, Poland.

OPPOSITE A Jewish family in the Dutch city of Amsterdam on their way to a transit camp and ultimately to their deaths in the extermination centres in Nazi-occupied Poland. An estimated 106,000 Dutch Jews, among them the young diary-writer Anne Frank, died during the war.

THE WANNSEE CONFERENCE

The minutes of the notorious Wannsee conference, convened at a villa on Lake Wannsee in Berlin on 20 January 1942, where the new programme of deporting Jews to the east as part of a "final solution" was announced. (See translation on page 157.)

Geheime Reichssache!

166

30 Ausfertigungen
16. Ausfertigung

Besprechungsprotokoll.

I.   An der am 20.1.1942 in Berlin, Am Großen Wannsee Nr. 56/58, stattgefundenen Besprechung über die Endlösung der Judenfrage nahmen teil:

Gauleiter Dr. Meyer und Reichsamtsleiter Dr. Leibbrandt	Reichsministerium für die besetzten Ostgebiete
Staatssekretär Dr. Stuckart	Reichsministerium des Innern
Staatssekretär Neumann	Beauftragter für den Vierjahresplan
Staatssekretär Dr. Freisler	Reichsjustizministerium
Staatssekretär Dr. Bühler	Amt des Generalgouverneurs
Unterstaatssekretär Luther	Auswärtiges Amt
SS-Oberführer Klopfer	Partei-Kanzlei
Ministerialdirektor Kritzinger	Reichskanzlei

K210400   372624

- 2 -

167

SS-Gruppenführer Hofmann	Rasse- und Siedlungshauptamt
SS-Gruppenführer Müller SS-Obersturmbannführer Eichmann	Reichssicherheitshauptamt
SS-Oberführer Dr. Schöngarth Befehlshaber der Sicherheitspolizei und des SD im Generalgouvernement	Sicherheitspolizei und SD
SS-Sturmbannführer Dr. Lange Kommandeur der Sicherheitspolizei und des SD für den Generalbezirk Lettland, als Vertreter des Befehlshabers der Sicherheitspolizei und des SD für das Reichskommissariat Ostland.	Sicherheitspolizei und SD

II.   Chef der Sicherheitspolizei und des SD, SS-Obergruppenführer H e y d r i c h , teilte eingangs seine Bestellung zum Beauftragten für die Vorbereitung der Endlösung der europäischen Judenfrage durch den Reichsmarschall mit und wies darauf hin, daß zu dieser Besprechung geladen wurde, um Klarheit in grundsätzlichen Fragen zu schaffen. Der Wunsch des Reichsmarschalls, ihm einen Entwurf über die organisatorischen, sachlichen und materiellen Belange im Hinblick auf die Endlösung der europäischen Judenfrage zu übersenden, erfordert die vorherige gemeinsame Behandlung aller an diesen Fragen unmittelbar beteiligten Zentralinstanzen im Hinblick auf die Parallelisierung der Linienführung.

K210401   372025

- 3 -

Die Federführung bei der Bearbeitung der Endlösung der Judenfrage liege ohne Rücksicht auf geographische Grenzen zentral beim Reichsführer-⅏ und Chef der Deutschen Polizei (Chef der Sicherheitspolizei und des SD).

Der Chef der Sicherheitspolizei und des SD gab sodann einen kurzen Rückblick über den bisher geführten Kampf gegen diesen Gegner. Die wesentlichsten Momente bilden

a/ die Zurückdrängung der Juden aus den einzelnen Lebensgebieten des deutschen Volkes,

b/ die Zurückdrängung der Juden aus dem Lebensraum des deutschen Volkes.

Im Vollzug dieser Bestrebungen wurde als einzige vorläufige Lösungsmöglichkeit die Beschleunigung der Auswanderung der Juden aus dem Reichsgebiet verstärkt und planmäßig in Angriff genommen.

Auf Anordnung des Reichsmarschalls wurde im Januar 1939 eine Reichszentrale für jüdische Auswanderung errichtet, mit deren Leitung der Chef der Sicherheitspolizei und des SD betraut wurde. Sie hatte insbesondere die Aufgabe

a/ alle Maßnahmen zur Vorbereitung einer verstärkten Auswanderung der Juden zu treffen,

b/ den Auswanderungsstrom zu lenken,

c/ die Durchführung der Auswanderung im Einzelfall zu beschleunigen.

Das Aufgabenziel war, auf legale Weise den deutschen Lebensraum von Juden zu säubern.

K210402   372026

- 4 -

Über die Nachteile, die eine solche Auswanderungsforcierung mit sich brachte, waren sich alle Stellen im klaren. Sie mußten jedoch angesichts des Fehlens anderer Lösungsmöglichkeiten vorerst in Kauf genommen werden.

Die Auswanderungsarbeiten waren in der Folgezeit nicht nur ein deutsches Problem, sondern auch ein Problem, mit dem sich die Behörden der Ziel- bzw. Einwandererländer zu befassen hatten. Die finanziellen Schwierigkeiten, wie Erhöhung der Vorzeige- und Landungsgelder seitens der verschiedenen ausländischen Regierungen, fehlende Schiffsplätze, laufend verschärfte Einwanderungsbeschränkungen oder -sperren, erschwerten die Auswanderungsbestrebungen außerordentlich. Trotz dieser Schwierigkeiten wurden seit der Machtübernahme bis zum Stichtag 31.10.1941 insgesamt rund 537.000 Juden zur Auswanderung gebracht. Davon

vom 30.1.1933 aus dem Altreich   rd. 360.000
vom 15.3.1938 aus der Ostmark   rd. 147.000
vom 15.3.1939 aus dem Protektorat
           Böhmen und Mähren   rd. 30.000.

Die Finanzierung der Auswanderung erfolgte durch die Juden bzw. jüdisch-politischen Organisationen selbst. Um den Verbleib der verproletarisierten Juden zu vermeiden, wurde nach dem Grundsatz verfahren, daß die vermögenden Juden die Abwanderung der vermögenslosen Juden zu finanzieren haben; hier wurde, je nach Vermögen gestaffelt, eine entsprechende Umlage bzw. Auswandererabgabe vorgeschrieben, die zur Bestreitung der finanziellen Obliegenheiten im Zuge der Abwanderung vermögensloser Juden verwandt wurde.

K210403   372027

3 MARCH 1941–27 MARCH 1942

COMMANDO RAIDS: NORWAY TO ST NAZAIRE

In the summer of 1940, Churchill ordered the creation of a number of small units for raiding the enemy coast in Europe. The initial 11 battalion-size groups were known as commandos; each comprised 500 men who were highly trained for the dangerous task of breaching the German-held coastline and inflicting local damage or securing vital intelligence. No. 2 Commando would later become the Parachute Regiment. A Royal Marines officer, Lieutenant General Alan Bourne, was appointed Commander of Raiding Operations, charged with using the commando units for organized raids, but he was replaced almost at once by Admiral Roger Keyes. The first operations were minor raids in June and July 1940, but by 1941 the force was sufficiently prepared to begin more ambitious projects.

The most successful operations were mounted against the northern Norwegian Lofoten Islands on 4 March and 26 December 1941. The first of these netted valuable information to help crack the German navy's "Enigma" codes. The second was designed as a diversionary attack while another raid took place against the Vaagsö Islands in central Norway, on 27 December, where a small force, supported by naval gunfire, destroyed military installations and communications and captured 100 Germans for the loss of 19 commandos.

Larger and more significant raids were planned for the French coast at Bruneval and St Nazaire. Both were carried out under the new adviser on Combined Operations, Lord Louis Mountbatten. The first landing, on the night of 27–28 February, was designed to seize material from the new German Würzburg radar, which was used to control night fighters against British bombing attacks. The raid at Bruneval, near the French port of Le Havre, was mounted by a paratroop unit, which overcame the local German garrison, took parts of the radar and returned to Britain successfully across the Channel. The second attack, against the French port of St Nazaire, was a larger and more dangerous operation designed as part of the Battle of the Atlantic, which was reaching its height in the summer of 1942.

St Nazaire, on the French Atlantic coast, had the only dry dock large enough for the German battleship *Tirpitz*, which it was feared would use the base to raid Allied merchant shipping. An American-built destroyer, *Campbeltown*, made available to the British under the September 1940 destroyers-for-bases deal, was packed with explosives in its bow, and on the night of 27–28 March was sailed into the French harbour under the range of German guns. The destroyer avoided detection and rammed the dock's outer wall. A force of 268 commandos stormed the dock and destroyed equipment. The following day,

five tons of explosive blew up the dock wall, killing the Germans who had gone on board the destroyer and two captured commando officers (who had revealed nothing about the impending explosion). The raid took a heavy toll on the force – 611 took part, of whom 397 were casualties, including 144 killed – but the damage done was severe enough to justify the attack.

The success of the commando operations was mixed, but they became a regular feature of British warfare, a useful source of intelligence and a growing irritation to the German High Command. Following a raid on the Channel Islands on 3 October 1942, in which a number of bound German soldiers were killed, Hitler ordered that British and Canadian prisoners should be placed in shackles. On 18 October he issued a decree that any British commandos or special forces caught on raids were no longer to be treated as regular prisoners-of-war but were to be handed over to the German security forces for interrogation and punishment. The shackles were removed after the British had responded in kind on German prisoners, but Hitler's Commando Order stayed in place.

17 NOVEMBER 1941
Abortive Commando raid on Rommel's headquarters in North Africa.

1 FEBRUARY 1942
Vidkun Quisling appointed Minister President in Norway.

18 APRIL 1942
Pierre Laval becomes premier in Vichy France.

18 APRIL 1942
Doolittle air raid on Tokyo and other Japanese cities.

4 OCTOBER 1942
Commandos raid the Channel Island of Sark.

11–12 DECEMBER 1942
Commando raid against Axis shipping in the Gironde river in western France.

BELOW Men of "C" Company, 2nd Parachute Battalion, returning on a motor torpedo boat to Portsmouth on the morning following the Bruneval raid, 28 February 1942. The commander of the assault force, Major J D Frost, is on the bridge, second from left.

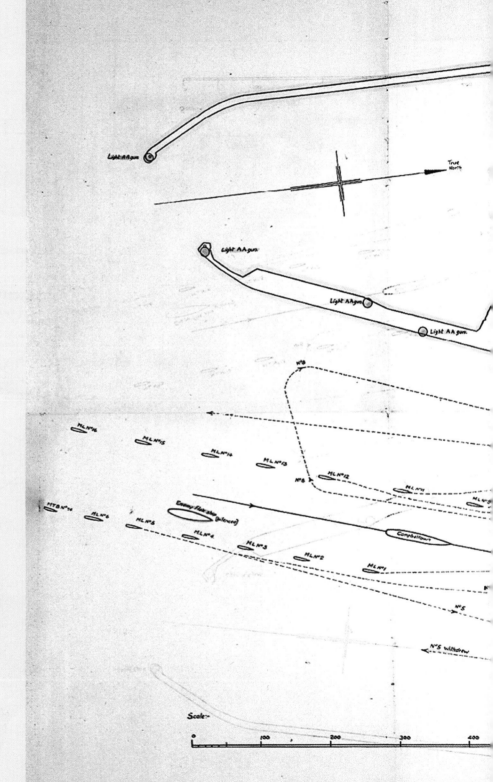

THE ATTACK ON ST. NAZAIRE
AT
0130 ON 28TH MARCH, 1942.

MAP OF ST NAZAIRE

A hand-drawn map of the raid on the
French Atlantic port of St Nazaire on the
night of 27–28 March 1942 showing the
route taken by the small British flotilla that
attacked the port. The map was drawn
a few days later, on 1 April 1942.

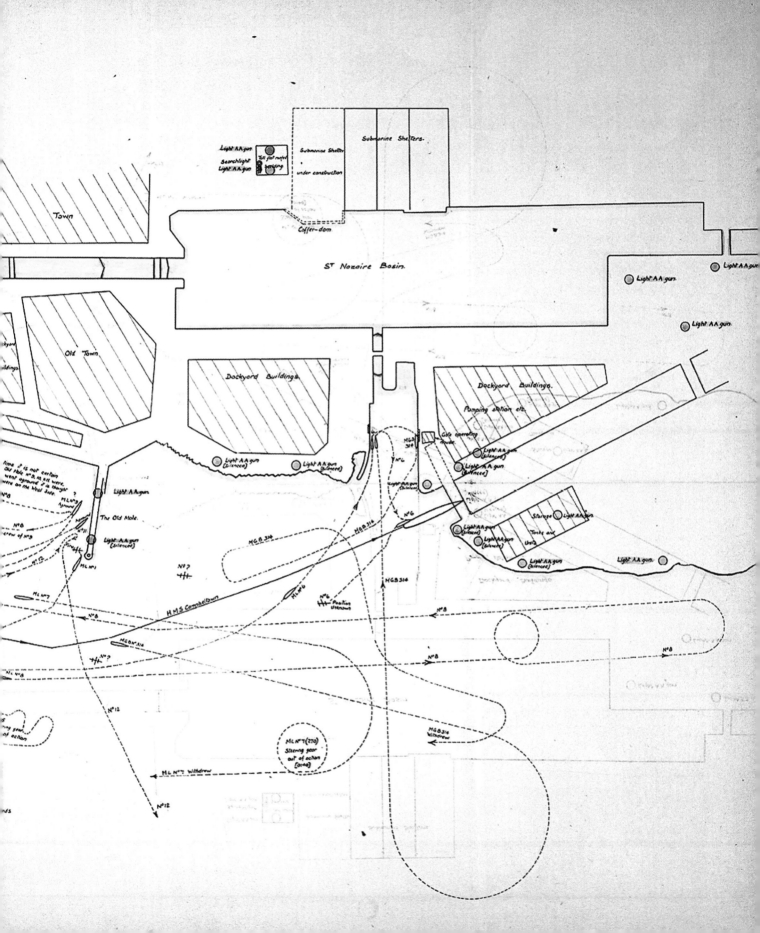

Town

Old Town

Submarine Shelters.

Submarine Shelter
under construction

Light A.A.gun
Searchlight
Light A.A.gun

1st flat rubel
building

Coffer-dam

St Nazaire Basin.

Light A.A.gun

Light A.A.gun

Light A.A.gun

Dockyard Buildings.

Dockyard Buildings.

Pumping station etc.

Caie operating
House

Light A.A.gun
(silenced)

Light A.A.gun
(silenced)

Light A.A.gun
(silenced)

Light A.A.gun
(silenced)

Light A.A.gun
(silenced)

Light A.A.gun
(silenced)

Light A.A.gun
(silenced)

Light A.A.gun
(silenced)

Light A.A.gun
(silenced)

Storage

Light A.A.gun

Tanks and
Units.

Light A.A.gun

M.G.B.314.

M.G.B.314.

M.G.B.314.

HMS Campbeltown.

M.G.B.314.

M.G.B.314
Withdrew.

The Old Mole.

Light A.A.gun

M.L.N°5
Aground

Light A.A.gun
(silenced)

M.L.N°1

M.L.N°7

No 7

N° 8

N° 8

N° 8

N° 8

N° 8

N° 12

N° 12

M.L.N°7 Withdrew

M.L.N°7 (270)
Steering gear
out of action
[0140]

M.L.N°6

N°6

N°6

N°6

N°6
Position
unknown

7–8 MAY 1942

CORREGIDOR: FALL OF THE PHILIPPINES

The only major United States presence in the western Pacific was in the Philippines, an island group south of Formosa (Taiwan), which had been taken over by the United States after the Spanish-American war of 1898, but which by 1941 enjoyed a semi-autonomous status under American supervision. The island group lay directly in the path of the Japanese assault on the oil and raw-material riches of Malaya and the East Indies. The Japanese planned to capture it within 50 days of the sustained air attacks on 8 December which signalled the start of their campaign. The forces opposed to the Japanese 14th Army under Lieutenant General Homma were a mixture of recently arrived American soldiers, some 30,000 strong, and five divisions of the poorly resourced Filipino army, numbering 110,000 men. The garrisons were scattered around the many islands of the archipelago, with the largest concentration on the island of Luzon. General MacArthur, the senior US commander, had tried to strengthen the air component of the Philippines defence, including the addition of 35 of the new B-17 "Flying Fortress" bombers, but the reinforcement of the region was not a high priority in Washington.

The surprise Japanese attack on 8 December was made from air bases in Formosa by specially trained pilots in aircraft modified to cope with the long cross-sea flight. The US aircraft on Luzon were almost all on the ground and undispersed. Half were destroyed in the first wave of attack, and more in the next two days. The battle for the Philippines was waged on the Allied side with no effective air power. Japanese air superiority also compelled the commander of the US Asiatic Fleet, Admiral Thomas Hart, to withdraw US naval shipping from the defence of Luzon. Small units of Japanese troops were landed over the following week, including a force on Mindanao, the main southern island in the group, where the air base at Davao was captured. On 22 December, the main body of Homma's force landed on either side of Luzon island in an attempt to encircle the enemy's forces around the capital, Manila. Bowing to reality, MacArthur ordered his forces to retreat to the Bataan peninsula on the southern flank of Manila Bay, and moved his headquarters to the island fortress of Corregidor at the seaward end of Bataan.

Although they were short of military supplies and food, the army units on Bataan greatly outnumbered Homma's force – which had totalled 43,000 at the start of the campaign – and they held up the conquest of the island for almost three months. High Japanese casualties and the withdrawal of a division to help in the conquest of the Netherlands East Indies forced Homma to halt and wear down the Filipino and American defenders by siege. By March, when MacArthur was ordered to leave the

4–8 MAY 1942
Battle of Coral Sea prevents Japanese conquest of southern New Guinea.

5 MAY 1942
Chinese mount attacks on Japanese-occupied cities.

5 MAY 1942
British Empire forces land on Madagascar.

15 MAY 1942
Japanese drive British Empire and Chinese troops out of Burma.

22 MAY 1942
Mexico declares war on the Axis Powers.

Philippines, it was evident to the defenders that there would be no aid or reinforcement. Lieutenant General Wainwright, who was given overall command by MacArthur following his own withdrawal to the safety of Australia, kept up a spirited defence, but when Homma attacked with fresh troops on 3 April the front collapsed, and on 9 April Major General Edward King, commanding the forces on Bataan, surrendered. Some 78,000 Filipino and American soldiers and civilians were taken captive and forced to walk 100 kilometres (65 miles) across the peninsula. The Bataan Death March, as it came to be known, saw atrocities routinely committed against prisoners already debilitated by hunger and disease.

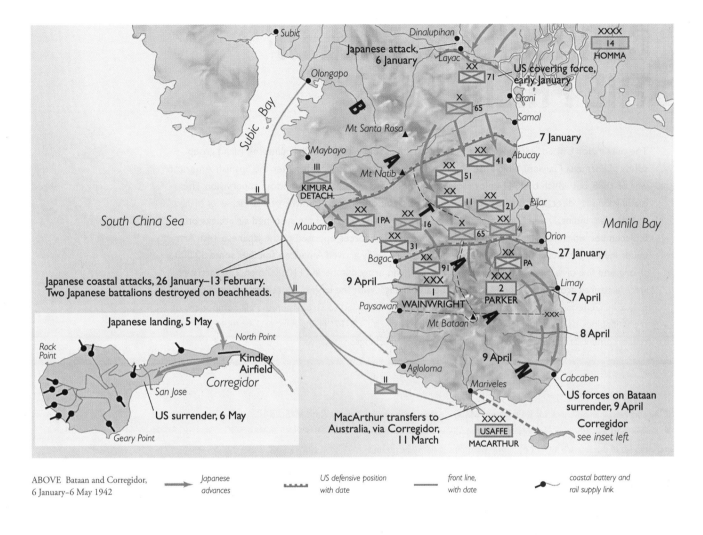

ABOVE Bataan and Corregidor,
6 January–6 May 1942

→ Japanese advances

⊓⊓⊓⊓ US defensive position with date

── front line, with date

●━ coastal battery and rail supply link

Map labels:
Subic
Dinalupihan
Japanese attack, 6 January
Layac
Olongapo
US covering force, early January
XXXX 14 HOMMA
XX 71
X 65
Orani
Samal
B
Mt Santa Rosa
7 January
Maybayo
A
XX 41
Abucay
South China Sea
III KIMURA DETACH.
Mt Natib
XX 51
II
T
XX 11
XX 21
Pilar
Mauban
XX 1PA
XX 16
X 65
XX 4
Manila Bay
Orion
XX 31
A
Bagac
XX 91
27 January
XX PA
9 April
XXX 1 WAINWRIGHT
XXX 2 PARKER
Limay
Paysawan
7 April
A
Mt Bataan
8 April
9 April
N
Agloloma
Cabcaben
Mariveles
US forces on Bataan surrender, 9 April
MacArthur transfers to Australia, via Corregidor, 11 March
XXXX USAFFE MACARTHUR
Corregidor see inset left

Japanese coastal attacks, 26 January–13 February.
Two Japanese battalions destroyed on beachheads.

Inset:
Japanese landing, 5 May
North Point
Rock Point
Kindley Airfield
Corregidor
San Jose
US surrender, 6 May
Geary Point

LIEUTENANT-GENERAL MASAHARU HOMMA
(1887–1946)

A successful career officer, Lieutenant General Homma had more understanding of the West than most Japanese commanders. He was a military attaché in London for eight years and was attached to British forces on the Western Front in 1918. He participated in the Japanese-Chinese war as a major general, and, despite his outspoken fears of the risks run by Japan, was chosen to command the Japanese 14th Army for the invasion of the Philippines. By May, the conquest was complete but the long delay in clearing the islands and Homma's liberal reputation disappointed the army leadership in Tokyo and he held no further operational commands for the remainder of the war. He was tried and executed in 1946 for atrocities committed by the troops under his command.

LIEUTENANT GENERAL JONATHAN WAINWRIGHT
(1883–1953)

Trained as a cavalryman, Lieutenant General Wainwright served in the First World War and in the inter-war years commanded cavalry units during the period of their transition to armoured warfare. In September 1940, he was made a major general and sent to command the Philippines Division, which he led at the start of the Japanese invasion. He was promoted to head the 1st Philippine Corps before being made overall commander-in-chief of forces in the Philippines after General MacArthur had left for Australia on 11 March 1942. He surrendered after the final struggle for the fortress of Corregidor and was imprisoned in Manchukuo, the Japanese puppet-state in Manchuria, where he was liberated by the Red Army in August 1945. He returned to a ticker-tape welcome in New York on 13 September 1945.

US troops surrender to the Japanese army on the Bataan peninsula in April 1942. Around 78,000 American and Filipino soldiers went into captivity, where thousands died from overwork, disease and violent mistreatment.

Around 2,000 soldiers had escaped to join the garrison in Corregidor and here Wainwright made his last stand with a total of 11,000 men. The system of deep tunnels under the fortress housed extensive stores and offered protection to the defenders. But relentless Japanese aerial and artillery bombardment destroyed almost everything on the surface, including most of the heavy guns, and on 5 May Homma's 14th Division landed on the fortress island itself. On 6 May, Wainwright surrendered to avoid further losses, and the following day announced the surrender of all forces throughout the Philippines. Fighting nonetheless continued as Japanese forces occupied all the outer islands. Some Filipinos escaped into the mountains to become guerrilla fighters. Forces on Negros only surrendered on 3 June and on Samar by 9 June, bringing the conquest of the islands to an end. By this time, almost the whole southern region was in Japanese hands.

20 JANUARY–16 JUNE 1942

JAPAN CONQUERS BURMA

The conquest of most of Burma by Lieutenant General Shojiro Iida's Japanese 15th Army in the first five months of 1942 represented the furthest limit of Japanese westward expansion. Burma became important to Japanese planners as a means to interrupt the flow of resources along the "Burma Road" to the Chinese armies they were fighting and to the area already conquered in south-east Asia, with its rich material resources. Burma also possessed oil and significant supplies of the rare metal tungsten. Later, it was to be a possible stepping stone for the invasion of India.

Burma's sudden strategic significance was understood far too late by the British authorities who controlled the country in conjunction with a Burmese native administration established under the Burma Act of 1935. Many leading Burmese politicians were anti-British and pro-Japanese, and the nationalist Burma Independence Army, an organization of Burmese dissidents, waited in the wings. In late 1941, there were around 27,000 British and Empire troops in Burma, 15,000 of whom were Burmese, organized into frontier forces and the 1st Burma Infantry Division formed in July 1941. The great bulk of remaining forces were Indian troops, officered by the British. There was little artillery, and only 32 aircraft. When General Iida's 15th Army attacked with two under-strength divisions on 19 January 1942, Japanese aircraft, operating from airfields captured in December, had already inflicted heavy damage on the capital Rangoon and other military targets. Resistance was limited and when the Indian 17th Division, defending Rangoon, was isolated on the wrong side of the Sittang River after the bridge was blown up prematurely, the Allied front collapsed. Some 3,484 Indian soldiers succeeded in crossing the river, but all their equipment was abandoned. The British 7th Armoured Brigade, newly arrived at the port, had to disembark and move almost

25 JANUARY 1942
Thailand declares war on Britain and the United States.

10 MAY 1942
Roosevelt announces dispatch of US troops to Greenland.

26 MAY 1942
Axis forces begin attack on Gazala line to force Allies back into Egypt.

27 MAY 1942
Himmler's number two, Reinhard Heydrich, mortally wounded by Czech agents. Men of Lidice and Ležáky murdered in retaliation on 10 June 1942.

28 JUNE 1942
Axis armies begin Operation "Blue" towards the Don steppe and the Caucasus.

2 JULY 1942
Churchill faces a vote of no confidence in the House of Commons but wins it by 476 votes to 25.

at once into combat. Further reinforcement proved impossible and over the following two weeks Japanese forces converged on Rangoon from the north and captured the city on 8 March.

VISCOUNT WILLIAM SLIM
(1891–1970)

Most of Field Marshal William Slim's soldiering was conducted in India and the Middle East following service at Gallipoli (where he was severely wounded) during the First World War. A brigadier in the Indian Army by 1939, he commanded an Indian army brigade in the conquest of Italian East Africa and then led the Indian 10th Division in the capture of Syria in June 1941. His powerful presence and popularity with his troops led to his appointment in March 1942 as commander of the Burmese Corps to try to stem the tide of Japanese advance through Burma. He orchestrated a successful retreat and later, in command of the 14th Army, he drove the Japanese back again across Burma in 1944. He was made a full general in 1945 and field marshal in 1949 while serving as Chief of the Imperial General Staff. He later served as Governor of Australia from 1953 to 1960, and ended his career as Governor of Windsor Castle.

Indian army troops and vehicles outside the Burmese town of Pyinmana, which was bombed by Japanese aircraft in an incendiary attack in April 1942, shortly before the British decision to abandon Burma.

British Empire forces were fortunate not to suffer a similar fate to the defenders of Malaya. Extricating themselves from almost certain Japanese encirclement before Rangoon was captured, the Burma Corps, created on 19 March and placed under the command of Lieutenant General Slim, retreated in fighting order much of the length of the Irrawaddy river valley running through central Burma, reaching the Indian town of Imphal in late May after a hazardous trek through jungle, plain and mountain. Japanese forces, supported by units of the Thai army and members of the Burma Independence Army, moved rapidly east and north, cutting off communications with the Chinese army, whose 38th Division fought alongside Burmese and Indian troops in an effort to keep the Japanese away from the north of the country. On 29 April, the decision was taken by the British authorities to abandon Burma, and Chinese forces in the north retreated back into Yunnan province. The Japanese army reached the Chinese border by 17 June and captured the airfield at Akyab, on the Bay of Bengal, on 4 May. Over the following months, Japan consolidated

control of the region but, with British Empire forces entrenched at Imphal, and after a gruelling six-month campaign, no effort was made to push on further into India.

The Japanese occupiers allowed the Burma Independence Army to rule parts of the country after the expulsion of the British, and Burma was nominally granted "independence" in August 1943, when the Burmese premier, Ba Maw, declared war on the Allies – the last state to do so. Japan nevertheless controlled the economy of the region and in reality acted as an occupying power with a significant garrison to guard the outer reaches of the new Japanese empire.

OPPOSITE A brick blast-proof bomb shelter under construction in the Burmese capital of Rangoon as protection against Japanese bombing. Heavy air attack began in January 1942, rendering the port almost unusable.

ABOVE Japanese tanks and infantry cross a bridge somewhere in Burma in June 1942 after completing the defeat of British Empire and Chinese forces. The Japanese tanks were poorly armed and armoured compared with European tanks, but there were few Allied tanks to defend Burma in 1942.

THE FIRST THOUSAND-BOMBER RAID

The bombing of German cities began in May 1940 and continued, when weather permitted and the forces were available, through to almost the last days of the war. The early attacks were made with low performance twin-engined bombers with small bomb loads flying at night, many of which found it difficult to locate even the town they were supposed to attack. The arrival of the Vickers Wellington medium bomber in larger numbers in 1941 and 1942 made it possible to mount more significant raids, but the problem of scale and accuracy persisted. When Arthur Harris was appointed as Commander-in-Chief Bomber Command in February 1942, support for the bombing campaign was growing thin. A report based on investigation of photo-reconnaissance in the autumn of 1941, known as the Butt report after the civil servant who drew it up, showed that only 20 per cent of aircraft actually attacked the 195 square kilometres (75 square miles) surrounding a designated target.

Harris set out to reinvigorate the bombing campaign and to show the politicians in Britain and the United States that bombing was a worthwhile strategy. His campaign was based on a directive issued by the Air Ministry on 14 February, before he took command, which detailed a list of German industrial cities as targets for what came to be known as "area bombing". Harris searched for an operation that would attract maximum publicity and in May decided on mounting a "thousand-bomber raid" against the western German city of Cologne. The operation was to bring together all available bomber aircraft, including those from the training schools, since there were only 400 operational bombers in frontline units. Instead of a cluster of bombers, Harris planned to use a bomber stream (in which all bombers flew at a single speed on a common route to the target, so overwhelming the defences), which was made possible by the introduction of a new navigation device, first used in a minor attack against Cologne on 13 March, known as Gee (ground electronics engineering). Leading aircraft guided by the radio beam dropped flares and incendiaries to illuminate the target, while the bombers that followed dropped their bombs on the burning area one after the other. The result was a much larger concentration of more accurate bombing.

The attack was planned for 27 May but had to be postponed because of poor weather. Finally, after four days of waiting on alert, the crews were ordered to fly off on 30 May. The Gee-guided bombers found and illuminated the target and of the 1,047 aircraft assembled some 868 bombed the city. The attack resulted in the death of almost 500 people

8 FEBRUARY 1942
Albert Speer appointed Minister of Weapons and Munitions to rationalize the German war economy.

14 FEBRUARY 1942
Air Ministry directs RAF Bomber Command to begin programme of area bombing.

23 FEBRUARY 1942
Arthur Harris appointed to take over as Commander-in-Chief Bomber Command.

14 APRIL 1942
Hitler authorizes "Baedeker" raids on British cities in retaliation for destruction of German ports.

8 APRIL 1942
One of the heaviest RAF attacks of the war so far, against Hamburg.

1 JUNE 1942
Heavy German "Baedeker" attack on the Kent cathedral city of Canterbury.

LEFT Air Gunner's Badge.

OPPOSITE RAF ground crew preparing to arm a Vickers Wellington bomber with a 4,000lb bomb on 27 May 1942 at the bomber base at Mildenhall, Suffolk. Poor weather postponed the planned attack on Cologne for four days.

AIR MARSHAL ARTHUR HARRIS
(1892–1984)

Arthur Harris became the best-known of Britain's RAF commanders during the war as a result of his prosecution of the bombing campaign against Germany between 1942 and 1945. He was the son of an Indian Civil Servant who chose in 1908 to go out to Rhodesia to make his mark. He joined the 1st Rhodesian Regiment in 1914, but in 1915 came to Britain to join the Royal Flying Corps. He served in the inter-war RAF in Iraq, India and Palestine, and in September 1939 was appointed commander of No. 5 Bomber Group. In 1941, he became an air marshal and on 21 February 1942 commander-in-chief of Bomber Command. He conducted a ruthless campaign of bombing against German industrial cities. His conviction that this was the efficient key to victory made him a difficult collaborator when bombers were needed for other tasks. He was made a marshal of the Royal Air Force in 1945, and fought a long conflict with the critics of bombing in the years that followed.

and the destruction of 13,010 dwellings, but did not seriously affect the industrial activity of the city. In all, 41 aircraft were lost to anti-aircraft fire and accident. Two days later, 956 bombers attacked the Ruhr city of Essen, and on 25 June 960 were assembled for an attack on the port of Bremen, but neither attack created serious levels of damage. In retaliation for earlier heavy raids on Lübeck and Rostock, the German air force launched the so-called Baedeker raids (an official in Berlin announced that British cities with three stars in the Baedeker tourist guide would be targeted) at the same time, killing 1,637 people in raids on Exeter, Norwich, Bath, York and Canterbury.

Harris achieved part of his purpose and bombing remained a central element in Britain's war effort, but the thousand-bomber raids were considered an extravagant use of scarce aircraft and more modest operations were planned thereafter, with increased bomb-load made possible by the introduction of the heavy Avro Lancaster, Short Stirling and Handley-Page Halifax bombers during the course of 1941 and 1942. In 1942, however, Bomber Command, joined by the bombers of the US 8th Air Force, released only 2.7 per cent of the total weight of bombs dropped throughout the whole war in Europe.

LIEUTENANT GENERAL JOSEF KAMMHUBER
(1896–1986)

A farmer's son from Bavaria, Josef Kammhuber volunteered for war service in 1914 and saw action at the siege of Verdun. He helped to train German pilots secretly in the Soviet Union in the late 1920s and was taken into the new air force after 1935 as a staff officer, returning to active duty in February 1939. He was shot down in the Battle of France but freed a few weeks later. In July he was made the commander of the first night-fighter division and given overall responsibility for the German air defence network, which came to be called the "Kammhuber Line". After a disagreement in late 1943 with Göring's deputy, Erhard Milch, over a new night-fighter, Kammhuber was demoted to air commander in Norway. In February 1945, Hitler called him back as "Plenipotentiary for the Fight against Enemy Four-engined Bombers". In 1956, he became director of the air force department in the German Defence Ministry with the rank of Lieutenant General and retired in 1962.

LEFT A vertical aerial photograph taken during Operation "Millennium", the attack on Cologne, on 31 May 1942. The sky is illuminated by searchlights and tracer fire from anti-aircraft batteries, while the first bombs dropped can be seen on the lower left of the picture.

OPPOSITE The stark ruins of the city of Cologne at the end of the war in 1945. Although badly hit during Operation "Millennium" most of the damage to the city was sustained in more than 200 raids experienced between 1942 and 1945.

4–5 JUNE 1942

THE BATTLE OF MIDWAY

The Japanese failure at the Battle of the Coral Sea confirmed the navy commander-in-chief, Admiral Isoroku Yamamoto, in his conviction that a decisive action should be taken against the United States Pacific Fleet to prevent further American activity in the western Pacific area. The tiny island of Midway, lying between Hawaii and Japan, was chosen as the target, not because it was important in itself, but as the lure to obtain the decisive fleet engagement which would eradicate the American threat. Preparations for Operation "MI" began in early May, just before the Battle of the Coral Sea.

Midway was claimed by the United States in 1859, occupied in 1903 and finally turned into a small naval and flying-boat base in 1940. The naval force sent across the Pacific from Japan was vast for the invasion of a small island, but that was not its principal purpose. The Japanese fleet was divided into five attacking groups: a carrier strike force, the heart of the operation, under the command of Vice Admiral Nagumo; an occupation force for Midway; the main battle fleet of seven battleships, including Yamamoto's huge flagship, the 72,000-ton *Yamato*, designed to eliminate the American fleet; a diversionary force to capture two of the Aleutian Islands in the north; and finally a forward screen of submarines. The date for the attack on Midway was set for 5 June Japanese time, 4 June in the United States. Japanese intelligence on the United States carrier force was scanty, but it was assumed that the two remaining carriers after the Battle of the Coral Sea were far away to the south, protecting Australia.

This was the first of the Japanese miscalculations. Nimitz had two carriers, *Hornet* and *Enterprise*, and thanks to an extraordinary technical feat of repair, the damaged *Yorktown* was also available by 31 May. The force was placed under the overall command of Admiral Fletcher, and the carriers placed under Rear Admiral Raymond Spruance. Against the Japanese four carriers, seven battleships, 12 cruisers and 42 destroyers, the Americans could muster only three carriers, eight cruisers and 15 destroyers. The one solid advantage enjoyed by the American side was intelligence, and without it the battle could not have been fought and won. The Fleet Radio Unit Pacific at Pearl Harbor could decode and decipher the Japanese main code, JN-25, and knew by 22 May that Operation "MI" meant Midway. A few days later, the time for the attack on Midway and the Aleutians was also known. The American strategy was to sail the small carrier force northeast of Midway, out of range of Japanese search aircraft and submarines. Once the Japanese units had been identified by aircraft from Midway, the plan was to assault them with

ABOVE US navy Dauntless dive-bombers attacking units of the Japanese fleet during the Battle of Midway. In the centre of the picture can be seen a burning Japanese cruiser, *Mikuma*, which had collided with another Japanese ship. The dive-bombers were responsible for the devastating damage suffered during the battle by the four Japanese carriers.

waves of torpedo- and dive-bombers but at all costs to avoid the big fleet engagement sought by Yamamoto.

The battle represented a great risk for the American side, heavily outnumbered in ships and aircraft, but the failure of Japanese reconnaissance

25 MAY 1942

Small Japanese fleet leaves Hokkaido island bound for the Aleutians off the coast of Alaska.

27 MAY 1942

USS *Yorktown* returns to Pearl Harbor for repairs following Coral Sea battle.

5 JUNE 1942

United States declares war on Hungary, Bulgaria and Romania.

7 JUNE 1942

German army begins final assault on Crimean port of Sevastopol.

11 JUNE 1942

German submarines begin a minelaying programme in US coastal waters.

12 JUNE 1942

Anglo-Soviet agreement on creating a "Second Front" published.

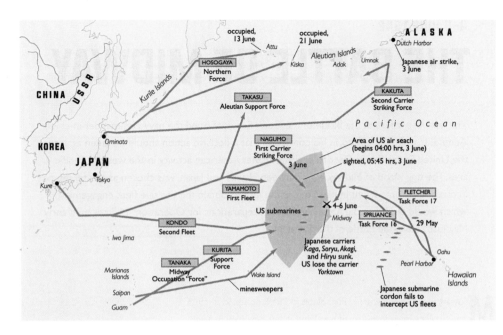

ABOVE The Battle of Midway, 24 May–6 June 1942. Japanese admiral Yamamoto's lavish assault plans for Midway foundered when he miscalculated the size and position of the American carrier forces, leading to a disastrous defeat.

→ Japanese fleet advance

→ US fleet advance

to detect Spruance's force until well after the attack on Midway had begun left the Japanese carriers exposed to a dangerous counter-attack as their aircraft were refuelled and rearmed on deck. The American torpedo-bombers were too slow and the force was decimated, but around 50 Dauntless dive-bombers, undetected by the Japanese, dropped enough bombs onto the carriers' crowded decks to create havoc. By early next morning all four Japanese fleet carriers, *Hiryu*, *Kaga*, *Soryu* and Nagumo's flagship, *Akagi*, were sunk. Yamamoto ordered his battleships forward to destroy the enemy but in thick fog they could not be found, and without

air cover the ships faced a great risk. *Yorktown* was damaged by aircraft, and sunk by a submarine three days later, but the great fleet engagement eluded the Japanese. The American victory was decisive, and it was achieved in a battle conducted and won by aircraft from two carrier forces that never even sighted each other. Senior Japanese commanders later admitted that this was the turning point in Japan's war effort. In 1943 and 1944, Japanese shipyards turned out another seven aircraft carriers; the United States built 90. The death and injury of 70 per cent of Japan's highly trained naval pilots was never satisfactorily made good.

ADMIRAL RAYMOND A. SPRUANCE
(1886–1969)

Admiral Spruance became a career naval officer before the First World War and by 1940 was commander of the Caribbean Sea Frontier. After the attack on Pearl Harbor he commanded Cruiser Division Five in the Pacific under command of Admiral William Halsey. Spruance – nicknamed "electric brain" – had a reputation for a sharp mind and cool temperament. When Halsey fell ill in May 1942, he recommended Spruance should control his carrier task force for the Battle of Midway. After the engagement he became Nimitz's Chief-of-Staff and in mid-1943 was appointed to command the Central Pacific Force which captured Iwo Jima and Okinawa. He succeeded Nimitz as commander of the Pacific Fleet in late 1945, and then became President of the Naval War College until his retirement in 1948. Between 1952 and 1955 he was US ambassador in the Philippines.

CAPTAIN JOSEPH ROCHEFORT
(1900–1976)

Captain Rochefort was one of the leading American experts on cryptanalysis. He joined the US navy in 1918, was trained in code-breaking and learned fluent Japanese. His wide intelligence experience led to his appointment early in 1941 to head the radio intercept office at Pearl Harbor. Here he assembled a large team of cryptanalysts and linguists who made it their task to break the Japanese naval code JN-25. During the early part of 1942 they succeeded in breaking the complicated cipher mechanism and could read some of the messages, although dates proved difficult. This intelligence information – known, like its European counterpart, as ULTRA – was vital for the Battle of Midway. The dating system was finally broken in May and Rochefort's unit provided the vital intelligence needed for the coming battle. From 1942 to 1946 he was in Washington as head of the Pacific Strategic Intelligence Group, and he retired in 1946.

BATTLE OF MIDWAY REPORTS

Official action reports from the US fleet after the Battle of Midway on 4–6 June 1942. The first provides an hour-by-hour account of the first day of the battle; the second provides a fuller account from the US aircraft carrier *Enterprise*.

PERTINENT EXTRACTS FROM COMMUNICATION LOGS RELATIVE TO MIDWAY ATTACK

3 June (zone plus 10)

LCT	GCT	FROM	TO	MESSAGE
1004	2104	Plane 6 of Flt. 55	Midway	2 Japanese cargo vessels bearing 247 470 I request instructions
1122	2122	Plane 7 of Flt. 55	Midway	Fired on strange cargo vessel bearing 258 distance 625 ships course 50 x I request instructions
1124	2124	Plane 8 of Flt. 55	Midway	Main body.
1209	2209	Midway	Plane 8 of Flt. 55	Amplify report of main body.
1240	2240	Plane 8 of Flt. 55	Midway	6 ships in column.
1249	2249	Midway	Plane 8 of Flt. 55	What type curse and speed
1322	2332	Midway	Plane 8 of Flt. 55	Return to base.
1806	0406	Cdr.Flt. 372	Midway	Investigate suspicious vessels. Contact bearing 261 distance 700
1812	0412	Cdr.Flt. 312	Midway	2 enemy destroyers 2 cargo vessels course 20 speed 13
2003	0603	Plane 6 of Flt. 92	Cdr.Flt. 92	Attacked alone bombs 1 troop transport afire

4 June (zone plus 10)

LCT	GCT	FROM	TO	MESSAGE
0406	1406	Plane 3 of Flt. 44	Midway	Am beign attacked by aircraft.
0407	1407	Plane 4 of Flt. 44	Midway	Attacked - - enemy bearing 260 distance 500.
0416	1416	Plane 4 of Flt. 44	Midway	Resume search.
0447	1447	Plane 13 of Flt. 44	Midway	Large enemy force bearing 261 distance 500 course 080 attacked with torpedoes attacked by aircraft I am returning to base.
0455	1455	Plane 2 of Flt. 44	Midway	Attack completed main body.
0512	1512	Plane 4 of Flt. 210	Midway	Affirm.
0514	1514	Plane 1 of Flt. 44	Midway	Attack completed hit large transport bearing 260 distance 500 enemy speed 13 oourse 080 10 ships.
0633	1633	Flt. 44 OC	Flt. 44	Identify enemy plane disposition report result.
0642	1642	COFlt 92	Flt. 92	Attack immediately.
0723	1723	Plane 4 of Flt. 58	Midway	Aircraft sighted.

- 1 -

LCT :	GCT:	FROM	:	TO	:	MESSAGE
0728:	1728:	Plane 4 of Flt. 58	;	OinC Flt. 58	:	One engine seaplane.
0734:	1734:	Plane 4 of Flt. 58	:	OinC Flt. 58	:	Enemy Carriers.
0740:	1740:	Plane 4 of Flt. 58	:	OinC Flt. 58	:	ED 180 sight 320.
0753:	1753:	Plane 3 of Flt. 58	:	Midway	:	Many planes heading Midway bearing 310 distance 150
----:	----:	Plane 6 of Flt. 58	:	OinC Flt. 58	:	Twin float seaplane bearing 336 distance 148
0803:	1803:	OinC Flt. 92	:	OinC Flt. 58	:	2 carriers and battleships bearing 320 distance 180 course 135 speed 25
0807:	1807:	CTF 17	:	CTF 16	:	Proceed southwesterly and attack enemy carrier as soon as definitely located I will follow as soon as planes recovered.
0815:	1815:	CTF 16	:	TF 16	:	Prepare to launch aircraft.
0816:	1816:	CTF 16	:	TF 16	:	Go to general quarters.
0808:	1818:	OinC Flt. 44	:	Cdr. Flt. 44	:	Rendezvous hisianski.
0822:	1822:	CTF 17	:	CTF 16	:	Have you received report 2 CV and BB bearing 320 distance 180 miles from Midway course 135 speed 25 x This on 4265.
0834?	1834?	CTF 16	:	TF 16	:	At 0800 two enemy CV and BBs 30-30N Long 179-35W Course 135 speed 25.
0838:	1838:	Midway	:	All Aircraft	:	Air raid Midway.
0841:	1841:	Plane 4 of Flt. 58	:	OinC Flt. 58	:	I am returning to Pearl Harbor unless otherwise instructed.
0843:	1843:	Plane 11 of Flt. 55	:	Midway	:	Proceeding to Haysan Island.
0845:	1845:	CTF 16	:	Hornet and Enterprise:		Use deferred departure.
0846:	1846:	CTF 16	:	All ships this type	:	Launch aircraft at 0900.
0848:	1848:	CTF 16	:	Hornet	:	Midway planes have been sent to attack carriers.
0850:	1850:	Plane 1 of Flt. 55	:	Midway	:	I am proceeding to rendezvous.
0859:	1859:	OinC Flt. 55	:	Plane 5 of Flt. 55	:	Act at discretion.
0905:	1905:	Plane 5 of Flt. 55	:	OinC Flt. 55	:	I am proceeding Hisianski Island.
0909:	1909:	Plane 8 of Flt. 55	:	Midway	:	Fired at by small vessel course 085 bearing 264, true distance 340.
0920:	1920:	OinC Flt. 55	:	All stations this circuit.	:	Authenticate all transmissions on this circuit.

- 2 -

2

LCT :	GCT :	FROM	:	TO	:	MESSAGE
0930:	1930:	Plane 3 of Flt. 55	:	OinC Flt. 55	:	I am proceeding to Hisianski
					:	unless otherwise directed.
1027:	2027:	CTF 16	:	TF 16		Prepare to repel attack.
1038:	2038:	Plane 19 of Flt.55	:	OinC Flt. 55	:	4 CA enemy DDs, 2 tankers 2
					:	AP bearing 265 distance 400
					:	course 085.
1050:	2050:	OinC Flt. 23	:	Cdr. Flt. 23	:	Direct 3 patrol planes be
					:	vicinity Hermes 1500 report.
1057:	2057:	Cdr. Flt. 92	:	OinC Flt. 92	:	Attack completed on carrier
					:	one damaged is it clear to
					:	land.
1105:	2105:	Plane 9 of Flt. 55	:	OinC Flt. 55	:	8 enemy cruisers course 080
					:	bearing true and distance from
					:	ships previous report 320
					:	miles (plane previous report
					:	was bearing 265)
1114:	2114:	CTF 17	:	CTF 16	:	Launched three fourths of
					:	group at attack same carriers
1128:	2128:	-----	:	Midway	:	626 circling field your front
					:	wheel is not down bail out
					:	over lagoon.
1130:	2130:	Plane 3 of Flt. 4	:	Midway	:	No gas.
1138:	2138:	Plane 3 of Flt. 23	:	Cdr. Flt. 23	:	Radio compass out request
					:	bearing IFF.
1143:	2143:	Plane 4 of Flt.458	:	??	:	Bearing 357 distance 210.
1147:	2147:	OinC Flt. 92	:	Plane 16	:	Proceed to Midway immediately.
1154:	2154:	OinC Flt. 23	:	COFlt. 23	:	Proceed to Midway immediately.
1201:	2201:	Ent attack group	:	CTF 16	:	We have been over the enemy
					:	for the last half hour x 8 DD
					:	2 BB 2 CV.
1209:	2209:	Ent.	:	EAGC	:	Attack immediately.
1214:	2214:	CTF 16	:	CTF 17	:	Report received from entgroup
					:	cdr at about 1200 quote x No
					:	combat patrol over target x
					:	8 DDs 2 BBs 2 CVs course about
					:	north quote x my course 285.
1215:	2215:	EAGC	:	HAGC??	:	(Name could not identify)How
					:	about you take the one on the
					:	left I'll take the one on the
					:	right x I'm going to make an
					:	attack x you take the noodle
					:	over the left side I'll take
					:	the other one on the right.
1221:	2221:	CVB 6	:	VB 6	:	My div stay with me x I am
					:	going to over Gallaher may
					:	take next target.
1223:	2223:	Cdr. VB 6	:	----	:	1st div 2nd div stay with me
					:	and come on over - don't let
					:	this carrier escape.

CV6/A16-3/(60-Br) **U. S. S. ENTERPRISE**
(0133)

CONFIDENTIAL

At Sea,
June 8, 1942

From: The Commanding Officer.
To: The Commander-in-Chief, U.S. Pacific Fleet.

Via: Commander Task Force Sixteen.
     (Rear Admiral R.A. Spruance, U.S. Navy).

Subject: Battle of Midway Island, June 4 - 6, 1942 -
     Report of.

Reference: (a) Articles 712 and 874, U.S. Navy
       Regulations, 1920.

Enclosures: (A) Track Chart.
     (B) Photographs of enemy CA, damaged in
       the action of June 6, 1942.
     (C) Executive Officer's Report.

I. PRELIMINARY.

  1. On the afternoon and evening of June 3, 1942,
the general situation prior to the battle was as follows (times
throughout are Zone plus 10): Task Force Seventeen and Task
Force Sixteen had previously rendezvoused in the general vicinity
of "Point Luck", approximately 350 miles northeast of Midway
Island and were operating in that area closing Midway during
darkness and opening during the day, remaining east of the
longitude of Midway. Both Task Forces had completed fueling
to capacity and the oilers despatched to their rendezvous. The
Senior Officer Present Afloat and Officer in Tactical Command
was in YORKTOWN. The two task forces were separated but were
within visual contact. They were operating independently but
generally conforming in their movements. At 2150 course was
changed to 210°T. toward a 0630, June 4, rendezvous (31° 30' N;
176° 30' W) designated by Commander Task Force 17. At 1812
a radio message from Flight 312 to Radio Midway was intercepted
"2 enemy destroyers 2 cargo vessels course 020 speed 13".

  2. At 2000, June 3, 1942, ENTERPRISE, Flagship of
Commander Task Force 16 was in position 33° 16' N, 175° 46' W,
in the center as guide of Cruising Disposition 11-V, axis 270°T,
course 100°T, speed 15 knots and zigzagging according to Plan
Number 7. Wind south 9, clouds cumulus 7, visibility 30,
sea smooth.

- 1 -

CONFIDENTIAL

At Sea,
June 8, 1942.

Subject: Battle of Midway Island, June 4 - 6, 1942,-
Report of.
- -

3.   The following significant messages were received
during the night of June 3 - 4:

At 0447 - from Flight 44 to Radio Midway "large enemy
forces bearing 261°T, distance 500 course 080 speed 13 x
ten ships".
At 0734 - from Flight 58 to Radio Midway "enemy carriers".
At 0753 - from Flight 58 to Radio Midway "many planes
heading Midway bearing 320 distance 150".
At 0803 - from Flight 92 to Radio Midway "2 carriers and
battleships bearing 320° distance 180 course 135 speed 25".
At 0807 - from Commander Task Force 17 to Commander Task
Force 16 "proceed southwesterly and attack enemy carriers
when definitely located".   - No amplification

II. THE ACTION.

June 4, 1942. Wind SE 5, clouds cumulus 4, visibility 50,
sea smooth.

Time

0906 - Commenced launching attack group of 33 VSB, 14 VT, 10 VF.
             15 VSB armed with one 1000 lb. bomb each.
             12 VSB armed with one 500 lb. bomb and two
                  100 lb. bombs each.
              6 VSB armed with one 500 lb. bomb each.
             14 VTB armed with torpedoes.
1015 - Type 97 enemy twin-float seaplane sighted bearing 180°T.,
distance 72,000 yards. Combat Patrol failed to find
this plane although radar and lookouts confirmed its
position.
1129 - 1132 - Launched 8 VF for second Combat Patrol.
1145 - 1152 - Landed first Combat Patrol 8 VF.
1202 - Commander ENTERPRISE Air Group sighted Japanese Force
composed of 4 CV, 2 BB, 4 CA, 6 DD.
1220 - VT commenced attack; probably one hit on CV.
1222 - VSB commenced dive bombing attack; two (2) CV badly
damaged with many direct bomb hits, left in flames.
Position of enemy force, Lat. 30° 05' N, Long. 178° 50' W.
1244 - 1247 - Launched 8 VF for third Combat Patrol.
1255 - Commenced landing VF escort.

A 2

- 2 -

CV6/A16-3/(60-Br)   **U. S. S. ENTERPRISE**
   (0133)

At Sea,
                                                June 8, 1942.

Subject: Battle of Midway Island, June 4 - 6, 1942 -
                Report of.
- -

1316 - 1329 - Landed second Combat Patrol 8 VF.
1337 - 1340 - Launched 8 VF, fourth Combat Patrol.
1405 - 20 enemy planes reported bearing 310° coming in.
        (Attack on YORKTOWN followed).
1410 - Completed landing attack group.
1433 - 1435 - Launched 8 VF, fifth Combat Patrol.
1437 - 1438 - Landed 5-B-3 and 5-B-16 (YORKTOWN planes).
        YORKTOWN pilot reported YORKTOWN in bad shape. Heavy
        smoke seen from YORKTOWN.
1442 - 1448 - Landed 5-B-7, 5-B-8, 5-B-9, 5-B-10, 5-B-12, 5-B-14,
        5-B-15 (YORKTOWN planes).
1451 - 1459 - Landed 5-F-2, 5-F-3, 5-F-8, 5-F-21, 5-B-4, 5-B-5,
        5-B-6, 5-B-11, 5-B-13, 5-B-17 (YORKTOWN planes).
1504 - 1505 - Landed 5-F-10, 5-F-15 (YORKTOWN Planes).
1539 - 1541 - Launched 6 VF, sixth Combat Patrol.
1547 - 1559 - Landed third and fourth Combat Patrol, 16 VF.
1610 - VF shot down seaplane tracker 50 miles south of our force.
1645 - Received message from YORKTOWN scout, "1 CV, 2 BB, 3 CA,
        4 DD, 31° 15' N, 179° 05' W, course 000, speed 15."
1730 - Commenced launching second attack group composed of
        24 VSB.
                11 VSB armed with one 1000 lb. bomb each.
                13 VSB armed with one 500 lb. bomb each.
1742 - 1752 - Landed fifth and sixth Combat Patrols 10 VF.
        6-F-12 Mach. Warden missing and reported to have landed
        in water out of gas. Also landed 3 VF and 3 VSB from
        YORKTOWN. Landed 6-S-16 from Attack Group.
1835 - Combat Patrol (6-F-1 shot down 4-engine enemy seaplane).
1842 - 1846 - Launched 12 VF for ninth Combat Patrol.
1850 - 1852 - Landed 5 VF of seventh Combat Patrol. Also landed
        1 VF and 4 VSB from YORKTOWN.
1905 - Attacked Japanese Force composed of 1 CV, 2 BB, 3 CA, 4 DD,
        position Lat. 31° - 40' N, Long. 179° - 10' W. Left
        1 CV and 1 BB severely damaged and mass of flames.
1928 - 1930 - Landed 2 VF of eighth Combat Patrol and 1 VF from
        YORKTOWN.
1958 - 2005 - Launched 20 VF for tenth Combat Patrol.
2008 - 2034 - Landed 20 VSB of Attack Group. (3 did not return).
        Landed 9 VF of ninth Combat Patrol. Landed 2 VF of tenth
        Combat Patrol.
2034 - Completed landing attack group.

A 3

- 3 -

14–21 JUNE 1942

CRISIS IN EGYPT: GAZALA AND TOBRUK

The results of Operation "Crusader", which had pushed Axis forces back across the Western Desert to El Agheila by December 1941, were reversed almost as soon as they were achieved. Rommel, helped by the arrival of substantial supplies and reinforcements across the short Mediterranean supply route, launched a surprise counter-attack on 21 January 1942 which drove the tired British Empire forces more than halfway back to Egypt. The front stabilized at Gazala, where a line of strongpoints and minefields had been constructed stretching across the desert to the Free French garrison at Bir Hakeim. Neither side was in a position to take the initiative after months of combat in difficult conditions, and so the front stood firm at Gazala as both sides brought in reinforcements and fresh supplies of fuel and ammunition.

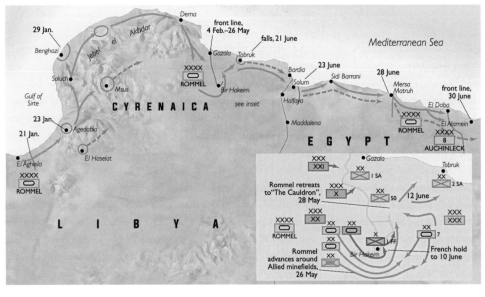

North Africa, 21 January–30 June 1942. Beginning in western Cyrenaica, over six months Rommel pushed back Allied forces all the way inside the Egyptian border and forced a decisive confrontation at El Alamein.

→ Axis advance   ⇢ Allied retreat
— Allied minefield

21 MAY 1942
Hitler decides to postpone invasion of Malta until the battle in Egypt is over.

30 MAY 1942
First thousand-bomber raid against Cologne by RAF Bomber Command.

31 MAY 1942
Japanese attack on Sydney harbour in Australia with three midget submarines. Three merchant ships sunk, 19 Australian and two Royal Navy sailors killed.

4–6 JUNE 1942
Battle of Midway results in first decisive victory for the Allies in 1942.

28 JUNE 1942
German summer offensive opens in the Soviet Union with drive to the Don steppe.

18 AUGUST 1942
Lieutenant General Bernard Montgomery takes command of the British 8th Army in Egypt.

The results of Operation "Crusader", which had pushed Axis forces back across the Western Desert to El Agheila by December 1941, were reversed almost as soon as they were achieved. Rommel, helped by the arrival of substantial supplies and reinforcements across the short Mediterranean supply route, launched a surprise counter-attack on 21 January 1942 which drove the tired British Empire forces more than halfway back to Egypt. The front stabilized at Gazala, where a line of strongpoints and minefields had been constructed stretching across the desert to the Free French garrison at Bir Hakeim. Neither side was in a position to take the initiative after months of combat in difficult

COUNT LÁSZLÓ ALMÁSY
(1895–1951)

The Hungarian aviator and explorer László Almásy became a counter-intelligence officer for Rommel's Afrika Korps in 1941. He fought as an airman in the Austro-Hungarian armed forces during the First World War, and made several attempts to restore the Habsburg dynasty to the throne after the collapse of the monarchy in 1918. He went to Egypt, where he became well-known as an explorer and map-maker of the desert regions of southern Libya. The Bedouin tribesmen named him "Father of the Sands"; he has become better-known as the model for the fictional "English Patient". When war broke out, he returned to Hungary, and was recruited by the German *Abwehr* (counter-intelligence) and posted to join Rommel in the desert war. He guided two German spies into Cairo in 1942 in Operation "Salaam", including Johannes Eppler, who set up the Condor spy-ring. In 1943, he fled to Turkey, where he continued to work for the *Abwehr*, but also for the British. He was tried for treason by the Hungarian Communist regime after the war, acquitted, and died in Vienna in 1951.

A German Focke-Wulf 190 fighter attacked and destroyed a British tank on the Via Balbia on 20 June 1942 during the British retreat across Libya.

conditions, and so the front stood firm at Gazala as both sides brought in reinforcements and fresh supplies of fuel and ammunition.

On 26 May, Rommel launched a renewed offensive. He had 560 tanks, almost half of them Italian, against a British Empire force of 700, recently reinforced with US-built Grant tanks. The Italian 10th and 21st Army Corps attacked the Allied front at Gazala in the north, while the bulk of Rommel's armoured forces swung south towards Bir Hakeim to try to encircle Ritchie's 8th Army. Although neither attack worked as Rommel had planned, the battle that followed showed how effective German armour could be in the hands of an imaginative commander. In the north, the Italian assault was held, while at Bir Hakeim, Free French forces offered stubborn resistance. Rommel was forced by 28 May to withdraw his forces, two German and two Italian armoured divisions, back into a defensive circle or "cauldron" (Kessel). Here he cleared minefields and with the help of "tank-busting" 88-milimetre (3.5-inch) anti-aircraft guns, repelled poorly co-ordinated attacks by British Empire forces from a zone codenamed "Knightsbridge" to the east of the "cauldron". By 1 June, Rommel was in a position to strike east in force and the Allied front crumbled. By 12 June, German armour and the Italian *Ariete* Division drove the enemy from Knightsbridge, while the Trieste Division was sent to help clear the French from Bir Hakeim, which finally succumbed on 10 June.

Unable to plug the gaps in the line, Ritchie ordered a retreat towards Tobruk, which was garrisoned by 35,000 troops, most of them South Africans. The 8th Army was unable to defend the port as it retreated in some disorder towards the Egyptian frontier, pursued by Rommel's armour. Tobruk was once again besieged but this time the defence was poorly organized, and by 21 June, after an assault of only three days, the fortress was taken and with it c.32,000 British Empire forces and their equipment and – from Rommel's point of view – vital supplies of fuel. The overall commander of British Empire forces in the Middle East, General Auchinleck, sacked Ritchie and took command himself. In order to avert complete disaster, which might have meant Axis control of the Suez Canal and access to the oil of the Middle East, Auchinleck abandoned the next defensive line further along the coast at Mersa Matruh, which was briefly contested between 27 and 29 June, for a more secure front at El Alamein and Alam Halfa, only 240 kilometres (150 miles) from Cairo. Though the scale was not the same as the struggle on the Russian steppe towards Stalingrad, there was a sense at Allied headquarters that the struggle for North Africa had reached its most critical stage. Axis armies here and in the Soviet Union seemed poised for victories that might turn the tide of war.

As Rommel's forces fast approached, the mood in Cairo worsened. Relations between the Egyptian population and the British Empire occupiers became increasingly strained, with food shortages and the sometimes disorderly behaviour of white troops. In February 1942, the British Resident Minister in Cairo had surrounded the royal palace with tanks and forced King Farouk to appoint a pro-British regime led by the Wafd Party. The King complied, but there remained important elements in the Egyptian military and political elite that waited expectantly for an Axis victory.

BATTLES OF GAZALA AND TOBRUK

A series of letters sent by Captain H. D. Lyttleton from North Africa on 4 September 1942 describing his experience in the battles of Gazala and Tobruk, which resulted in an Axis victory and pushed Allied forces back deep into Egyptian territory.

Capt. H.D. Lyttleton.
6th Bn Green Howards.
M.E.F.

4-9-42.

Dearest Falks, (No)

Mersa MATRU.

This afternoon I will try and take up the tale of our doings in the recent battles which I now feel are now sufficiently distant to allow of my writing about them.

I left off my tale I think when the Bn; in fact the whole Div, broke out of the Gazala line and withdrew inside the Egyptian Frontier. That was about the 14 or 15 June and I sent you a copy of the article in "Parade" called "Good old 50 Div" which gave an account of the operation.

The next incident that shook the 8th army no small amount was the fall of Tobruk within 24 hours of its being attacked. The Div promptly formed a force and was to act as a rear-guard and cover the withdrawal of 8 army to Matruh in the costal sector. For 2 or 3 days all was pleasant. We dug ourselves in near Sollum, and the forces infront of us withdrew through us without any trouble. Then the Bosche arrived on the scene and for 3 days we were on the move at night and holding positions by day. We were not directly attacked but the Bosche kept level with us on our flanks the whole time. On the first night the Bosch did get behind us and we were ambushed as the column moved back along the coast road. This cost us our signal officer and a DR, but we were too big a column to be stopped and it was only a small party that had filtered through and cut the road behind us.

"The following day we held positions about 20 miles West of Matruh, and a bad day it was too. The RAF had been given a wrong bomb line. A squadron of Kittybombers came over and we were just saying how nice to have some british planes about when down they came, dropped their bombs on us and proceeded to straff us from about 50 feet as there was of course no AA fire put up. Now we took a very poor view of that as you may imagine and said a few very hard things to the RAF over the wireless. But did that stop them? — Not at all. Twice more that day we were bombed and straffed by our own planes and I think any man in RAF uniform would have been murdered if he had been around that day.—

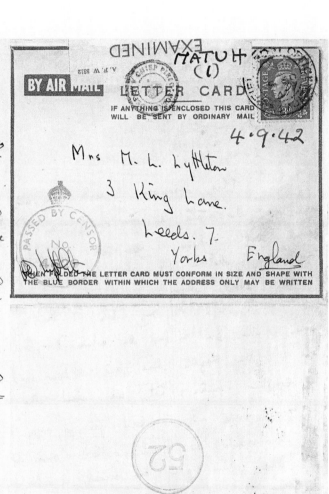

EXAMINED
A.F.W. 3312
MATUH
(1)

BY AIR MAIL LETTER CARD
IF ANYTHING IS ENCLOSED THIS CARD
WILL BE SENT BY ORDINARY MAIL

4·9·42

PASSED BY CENSOR
NO.

Mrs M. L. Lyttleton
3 King Lane.
Leeds. 7.
Yorks   England

WHEN FOLDED THE LETTER CARD MUST CONFORM IN SIZE AND SHAPE WITH
THE BLUE BORDER WITHIN WHICH THE ADDRESS ONLY MAY BE WRITTEN

52

Wt.38052/1894. 3,000,000. 12/39. S.J.P. 51-6531.

BY
BASE CENSOR

(Cont)

By evening the general situation was very sticky. A Bosch column had by-passed us to the south and bosch infantry were coming up the coast road. We were ordered to hold on until dark then withdraw along the main road into Matruh. The two obvious things happened. The Basche cut the coast road behind us and proceeded to attack us front & flank. So we settled down in our slit trenches and hoped for the best. Fortunately the attack was not pressed home before dark and we managed to get away by using a

track along the coast and left the Basche sitting happily astride the main road.

We got into Matruh that night and found organisational chaos reigning in a big way as it had been decided to hold the place only long enough to blow up the dumps etc. So that day found us in positions some 15 miles East of Matruh not knowing quite what it was all about or when someone was really going to sit down and say stop to the Basche.

The general position was that our armour had been so knocked about in the "Cauldron" and "Knightsbridge" that we had no force of tanks to stop the Basche in the desert and

so whenever infantry took up positions
the Bosch could just go round
our Southern flank and surround the
force, as he did in to the next
two days.

It was now about 26 June
when we were in position East of Matruh
in the coastal area. On the 27th the
Bosch by-passed us once more well
to the South and there was nothing
we could do about it. That night
however a very daring attack was
staged which if it had come off
would have made things very awkward
for the bosch.

The division was to go
due south x.x. behind the bosh and
attack his supply columns and cut
Me

down astride his supply route.

What a dirty night. First our gunners never turned up, so we had to leave without any guns. Then about 1.0 am we drove right into a basche leaguer. They opened up with every colour of tracer and flare they had and for a while chaos of the first water reigned. My wireless truck was hit and so I lost what little remained of my kit. We disentangled ourselves and debussed to put in an attack on foot. The attack it did a good bit of damage to the Bash but it was two big a leaguer for us without any arty support and the Bash are not the same proposition

as the Itis. In the end we withdrew our somewhat mauled forces and were ordered to return to the coastal area from which we started.

When we got back there on the morning of the 27th we found the situation had got pretty desperate. The basche had got round us in strength and had cut the road behind us good and proper, and believe me there was no small force inside that ring. The only answer was another break out that night. We were all absolutely buggered as you can well imagine and during that day we just lay about more depressed and dejected than I would have thought possible. In the afternoon the Bash
.

started shelling us but we just didn't bloody well care and I have never felt so indifferent as to what might happen.

Like the best serials I must leave you in the air just at the moment as to what did happen as I must do a spot of work now. I will finish my story anon and until the

Cheerio.

Tons of love.

Harry.

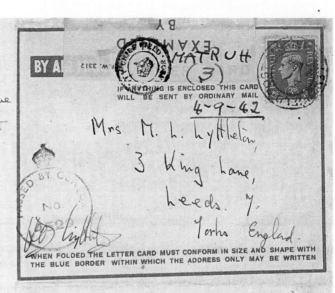

BY AIR

MATRUH (3)

IF ANYTHING IS ENCLOSED THIS CARD
WILL BE SENT BY ORDINARY MAIL

4-9-42

Mrs M. L. Lyttleton,
3 King Lane,
Leeds. 7,
Yorks England.

WHEN FOLDED THE LETTER CARD MUST CONFORM IN SIZE AND SHAPE WITH
THE BLUE BORDER WITHIN WHICH THE ADDRESS ONLY MAY BE WRITTEN

PASSED BY CENSOR
NO.
52

52

BY EXAMINED BY

444/PP & TJIJ 3,000 000 11/41

BY
BASE CENSOR

THE BATTLE OF THE ATLANTIC

On 6 March 1941, stung by the high losses of merchant ships to German submarines during the winter months, Winston Churchill announced that Britain was now fighting "the Battle of the Atlantic". The situation for the country was critical because so much of the raw material, oil and food the British war effort relied on, as well as the American aid promised through Lend Lease, had to be shipped across the Atlantic to British ports. In 1938, Britain imported 68 million tons of supplies, but in 1941 only 26 million. A total of 1,299 ships were lost to all causes in 1941 and the losses could not all be made good. By the spring of 1942, German naval commanders were convinced that Britain could be strangled into submission. So began a duel of the Royal Navy and the RAF against a force of around 300 German submarines under the command of Admiral Karl Dönitz, whose outcome was, as Churchill recognized, vital to the continued conduct of the war.

In the early months of 1942, following the entry of the United States into the war, German submarines, organized in packs with predatory codenames ("Leopard", "Panther" and "Puma") were sent to intercept American shipping. Unprepared for war, American ships were poorly equipped for anti-submarine warfare and could still be found sailing singly rather than in regular convoy. In the first four months of the year, 1.2 million tons of shipping was sunk off the American coast alone. Submarine losses were small: three in January, only two in February. The situation worsened over the year because the German B-Dienst intelligence unit had broken the British Naval Ciphers 2 and 3, directing convoy traffic across the Atlantic, while the British lost the knowledge they had gained from ULTRA when the German navy introduced the new Triton cipher in February. The Allies extended air patrols, forcing submarines into the so-called "Atlantic Gap" in mid-ocean, which aircraft could not reach, but here the submarines preyed on weakly escorted convoys or convoy stragglers. During 1942, seven million tons of shipping was lost in all areas, and by January 1943 the Royal Navy was dangerously low on fuel.

The situation might well have deteriorated further without the work of the British Admiralty's Submarine Tracking Room and Trade Plot Room, both located in London, which used a variety of intelligence sources to assess the submarine threat and to route convoys safely. In the year between May 1942 and May 1943, 105 out of 174 convoys sailed without loss. During 1942, the Allies introduced new technology and tactics to try to blunt the submarine threat. Better explosive charges, improved Air-to-Surface-Vessel (ASV) radar and the introduction of powerful searchlights, known as "Leigh lights" after their inventor, all increased the kill chances

12 JANUARY 1942
First ship sunk off the US East Coast by a German submarine.

5 JULY 1942
First German submarine sunk by aircraft using Leigh lights.

31 MAY 1942
Doenitz reports to Hitler that Atlantic battle is lost for the moment.

ADMIRAL MAX HORTON
(1883–1951)

Horton joined the Royal Navy in 1898 and had risen by the First World War to the rank of Lieutenant Commander in command of a submarine. He remained a submariner for the rest of the war, but in the inter-war years served on a number of battleships and reached the rank of Vice Admiral by 1939. In 1940, he was put in command of all home-based submarines. His experience made him an ideal choice to contest the German submarine arm, and on 17 November 1942 he was appointed Commander-in-Chief of the Western Approaches, responsible for the Battle of the Atlantic. His tactical innovations, particularly his use of free-ranging support groups to hunt down submarines on the edge of Allied convoys, played a critical part in turning the tide of the sea war. He was an avid golfer and was said to have played a round of golf almost every day of the war. He retired in August 1945.

against submarines. The accumulation of anti-submarine experience led to a sharp increase in sinkings during 1942 and forced the German submarines to operate in defined ocean areas.

In November 1942, with the appointment of Admiral Max Horton as Commander-in-Chief of the Western Approaches, which covered

Crew on board the US Coast Guard cutter *Spencer* watch as a depth charge blows a German submarine to the surface. The convoy they are protecting can be seen in the background.

the main area of the submarine battle, greater efforts were devoted to organizing well-trained and powerful escort groups to hunt out the submarines rather than simply protect the convoys. But in the absence of detailed intelligence, and without aircraft cover, it proved difficult to reform the battle quickly. During February and March 1943, in exceptionally poor weather, the submarine war reached a crescendo with the sinking of 21 ships in mid-Atlantic for the loss of just one submarine. Over the following few weeks, the battle suddenly turned abruptly in favour of the Allies. New escort carriers and Very Long Range Liberator aircraft were introduced to bridge the "Gap"; the Triton cipher was finally broken; and all aircraft were fitted with the new ASV Mark III radar and Leigh lights. In April, 15 submarines were sunk; in May, a further 41. German forces had no answer to the technical improvements, and on 24 May, Dönitz ordered submarines to retreat to their European bases, from which they continued to be attacked every time they ventured out to sea. In June 1943, not a single ship was lost in convoy and not a single attack reported. Although the submarine was not eliminated, the Battle of the Atlantic was effectively over.

THE VERY-LONG-RANGE AIRCRAFT

The Consolidated B-24 Liberator American heavy bomber played a critical role in the Battle of the Atlantic in helping to bridge the "Atlantic Gap" where it had been impossible to provide adequate air cover to track submarines. The aircraft only became available in March 1943, but with extra fuel tanks in the bomb bays and reduced armour it was possible for them to reach far out into the ocean from bases in Britain, Canada and Iceland. Armed with

centimetric radar and Leigh lights to illuminate submarines at night, Liberators were attributed 72 submarine "kills" during the course of the war.

ABOVE A Very Long Range (VLR) PB4Y-1 Liberator bomber flying over the Bay of Biscay during 1943 in the hunt for submarines.

7 AUGUST–27 OCTOBER 1942

BATTLE FOR THE SOLOMONS

After the Battle of Midway the Japanese continued with their plan to interrupt communications between the United States and the South Pacific by taking over a string of island bases east of New Guinea. At the southern end of the Solomon Islands group, on Guadalcanal, they landed a small force to construct an airfield, while they planned to use the nearby island of Tulagi as a small southern naval base. Allied intelligence on Japanese moves encouraged the decision to launch a pre-emptive attack on Tulagi and Guadalcanal with the object of neutralizing the Japanese threat to supply lines and breaching the perimeter of the southern area of their advance. Vice Admiral Frank Fletcher commanded the US naval force which arrived on 7 August, transporting 19,000 men of the 1st Marine Division under Major General Alexander Vandegrift. The landings on Guadalcanal resulted in the rapid seizure of the Japanese airfield at Lunga, while after two days of hard fighting the port of Tulagi was captured. The Japanese command, based further to the north in the New Britain port of Rabaul, reacted at once and Guadalcanal, a small tropical island covered with inhospitable jungle, became, like Midway, a battle over the limit of Japanese advance.

On the night of 8–9 August, a Japanese naval task force of seven cruisers and one destroyer arrived off Savo Island, in the strait between Lunga and Tulagi, where it sank four cruisers and damaged two more. Fletcher withdrew his carrier force, and over the next two weeks Japanese troops of the 17th Army under Lieutenant General Haruyoshi Hyakutake began to land on Guadalcanal. Although short of supplies and air support, the Marine force at what had been renamed by the Americans Henderson Field was able to repel the first Japanese attack by 21 August in the Battle of the Tenaru River. Japanese tactics were crude and the frontal assaults against men dug in with artillery and machine guns were suicidal. Almost all the 900 men in the first attack were killed for the loss of around 40 Americans. On 24 August, a second major Japanese naval force was sent south, but this time the naval battle that followed in the Eastern Solomons was more even. The Japanese carrier *Ryujo* was sunk by US carrier aircraft and although the US carrier *Enterprise* was damaged, the Japanese force withdrew. Nevertheless, the build-up of Japanese forces continued under cover of night. They were used for further attacks on the Henderson Field enclave, but all of them were repulsed, including the battle for "Bloody Ridge" on 12–14 September when the Japanese troops were annihilated once again. By mid-October, both sides had approximately the same number of forces – 22,000 Japanese and 23,000 Americans – while the presence of large Japanese naval forces posed a serious threat to the American foothold on the island.

The week beginning 23 October was potentially decisive. The Japanese army began a series of heavy attacks on Henderson Field, and on 25 October a light naval force bombarded the area and sank a number of small vessels. A major fleet engagement on 26 October off

OPPOSITE A group of US soldiers look at a map on a news board set up on the island of Guadalcanal. The fighting lasted from August 1942 to February 1943, during which time there was little respite from the combat.

22 JULY 1942
Japanese land at Gona and Buna on the southern peninsula of New Guinea.

12 AUGUST 1942
Japanese army begins major operation in Shantung province of China.

22 AUGUST 1942
Brazil declares war on Italy and Germany.

31 AUGUST 1942
Start of Battle of Alam Halfa in Egypt sees Rommel try to break Allied line.

5 SEPTEMBER 1942
Australian forces compel Japanese to abandon attack on Milne Bay in southern New Guinea.

3 OCTOBER 1942
First successful test launch of the German A4 rocket.

GENERAL ALEXANDER VANDEGRIFT
(1887–1973)

General Vandegrift joined the US Marine Corps in 1909, and after service in the Caribbean became a Marine Corps Assistant Chief-of-Staff; by 1940, assistant to the US Marine Corps Commandant, with the rank of Brigadier General. Shortly before Pearl Harbor he was sent to command the 1st Marine Division, and in May 1942 took the division to the south Pacific where he led it in the first full-scale invasion of Japanese-held territory in the Solomons. The capture of the island of Guadalcanal earned him the Medal of Honor and promotion to command of a Marine Corps. On 1 January 1944, he was promoted to Lieutenant General and became Commandant of the Marine Corps in Washington. In April 1945, he became the first Marine Corps officer to reach the rank of four-star General.

LIEUTENANT GENERAL HARUYOSHI HYAKUTAKE
(1888–1947)

A graduate from the Japanese Army Academy in 1909, whose fellow classmates included the future Chinese leader Chiang Kaishek, Hyakutake was sent in 1928 to the Kwantung Army in northern China, ending up on the general staff by 1935. After a number of field commands and training assignments he was chosen in May 1942 to command the Japanese 17th Army based at Rabaul in the south Pacific, and from here he orchestrated unsuccessful efforts to dislodge the American occupation of Guadalcanal. In the campaign in 1943 for the island of Bougainville he and his men were trapped in the interior and forced to live out the rest of the war there, hiding in jungle caves. After a serious stroke, Lieutenant General Hyakutake was relieved of duties in February 1945, but could not be evacuated to Japan until after the war was over.

the Santa Cruz Islands to the east of the Solomons led to the sinking of the US carrier *Hornet*, but also to heavy losses of Japanese carrier aircraft. The multiple attacks on Henderson Field over the period 23–26 October were once again repulsed with heavy losses in a series of hard-fought engagements, in which the two Marine divisions were joined by US army troops from the Americal Division. At the end of October, the situation was keenly balanced, but after three months of combat the US garrison had only succeeded in securing a small section of coast not much larger than the area they had first occupied

in August. Over the following weeks, the duel between Vandegrift and Hyakutake reached a bloody climax.

ABOVE Dead Japanese sailors in the campaign on Guadalcanal in the winter of 1942–3. Japanese forces lost 20,000 men in the unsuccessful attempt to hold on to the island.

OPPOSITE An aerial view of Henderson airfield on Guadalcanal in the Solomons in August 1944, some two years after US Marines assaulted the island and established a preliminary base there. The Lunga landing ground, renamed Henderson Field, was captured on 8 August and brought into operation by 21 August.

19 AUGUST 1942

THE DIEPPE RAID

When Lord Louis Mountbatten became Chief of Combined Operations in March 1942, he inherited plans for small-scale raids on German-held coastlines to test their defences and secure intelligence. Working together with the headquarters of the Home Army, Mountbatten and the Commanding Officer, South Eastern Command, Lieutenant General Bernard Montgomery, planned Operation "Rutter", a raid on the French port of Dieppe on the Channel coast. The raid was assigned to the Canadian 2nd Division, which was stationed in southern Britain, under the command of Major General John Roberts, and was to take place in July.

The purposes of the raid were not only operational. In the summer of 1942, there was strong pressure on the British War Cabinet from Moscow and Washington to show that Britain was capable of taking action against the German enemy. It was clear that no major cross-Channel invasion was possible in 1942 because of shortages of shipping and trained men, but the two men chosen to organize the raid, Mountbatten and the commander of No. 11 Group Fighter Command, Air Marshal Leigh-Mallory, were both strongly in favour of taking action against the enemy whenever possible. Leigh-Mallory had already organized what were called "Circuses", large groups of fighters with a few bombers to attack the north European coast and lure the German air force into battle. Mountbatten had already overseen the raids on St Nazaire and Bruneval.

9–10 AUGUST 1942
German army captures oil town of Maikop in the Caucasus region.

12 AUGUST 1942
Churchill arrives in Moscow for a conference with Stalin.

13 AUGUST 1942
The siege of Malta is relieved by the arrival of the convoy "Pedestal" in Valetta harbour.

17 AUGUST 1942
US Marines known as "Carlson's Raiders" successfully attack Makin Island, killing most of the Japanese forces there.

23 AUGUST 1942
Paulus's 6th Army reaches the Volga river to the north of Stalingrad.

A landing craft approaching the French shore during the Dieppe Raid of 19 August 1942 under cover of a smokescreen laid by RAF aircraft. The raid proved a disastrous gamble and alerted the Allies to the need for thorough preparation before a full-scale invasion.

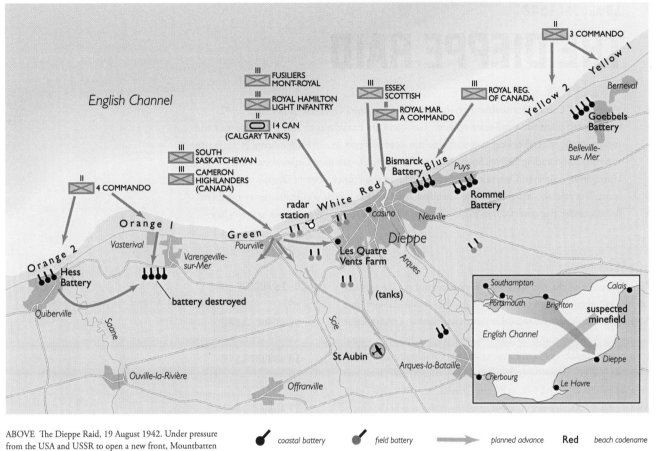

ABOVE The Dieppe Raid, 19 August 1942. Under pressure from the USA and USSR to open a new front, Mountbatten sanctioned a raid against Dieppe in France, but poor planning led to disastrous losses.

● coastal battery   ● field battery   → planned advance   **Red** beach codename

Operation "Rutter" was on a different scale, but when the time for the assault came the weather caused its cancellation and Montgomery assumed that the plan was finished. Mountbatten revived it under a new codename, Operation "Jubilee". No records of the plan were kept, but Churchill, the Canadian authorities and the head of the army had approved it and Churchill, the Chief of the Imperial General Staff, Mountbattan and Hughes-Hallett had seen the plans personally. The raid involved a total of 237 ships and landing craft, the Canadian Division, No. 3 and No. 4 Commandos, Royal Marine A Commando, 50 US Rangers and a total of 74 squadrons of aircraft, most of them fighters. This considerable force crossed the Channel on 19 August. Intelligence information was poor and the assault plan – for a frontal attack on the port – carried dangerous risks. Two flank attacks on the guns on either side of Dieppe were made by the commando units, but the one to the east was detected by a German convoy and the coastal garrison alerted. Only the batteries to the west were captured by No. 4 Commando. Half an hour after the flank attacks, at 5.20 in the morning, the main force landed on the port beaches under cover of a smokescreen. They came under heavy

AIR MARSHAL TRAFFORD LEIGH-MALLORY
(1892–1944)

Serving first in the army, then in the Royal Flying Corps in the First World War, Leigh-Mallory was commander of No. 12 Group RAF Fighter Command with the rank of Air Vice-Marshal when the war broke out. He argued during the Battle of Britain in favour of "Big Wing" tactics, using large numbers of fighters for a concerted attack on enemy bombers, but failed to convince his fellow commanders. As commander of No. 11 Group in 1942, he was responsible for fighter cover for the Dieppe Raid. He became Commander-in-Chief of Fighter Command in November 1942 and then commander of all tactical air forces for the Normandy landings. He was killed in an air crash in November 1944 on his way to take up a new command appointment in south-east Asia.

121

German soldiers inspect a destroyed British landing craft used during the raid on Dieppe. In all, some 33 landing craft and one destroyer were lost during the operation out of a total of 237 ships of all kinds used for the raid.

fire, and losses were high. Roberts called in his reserve forces to try to strengthen the assault, but the decision only compounded what was an evident disaster. The few tanks which were successfully landed either failed to scale the sea wall or were quickly immobilized in the town. By 11.00 a.m., the troops were ordered to withdraw and the evacuation of what was left of the force was completed by early afternoon.

The losses from the raid were exceptionally high. Out of the 4,963 Canadians, 3,367 were killed, wounded or captured. The total killed from all the forces committed was 1,027. The RAF lost 106 aircraft and destroyed only 48. The outcome had many causes, but the principal failure was not to recognize how difficult a frontal assault on a heavily defended port and coastline could be without prior bombing or naval gunfire, and with poor reconnaissance preparation. The lessons of Dieppe were absorbed in the later preparations for the landings in France, but the immediate impact was to rule out any prospect in the near future of a "Second Front" to help the Soviet war effort.

Stills from an airborne camera aboard a Spitfire Mark V as it engages and shoots down a German Do 217 bomber over the English Channel while escorting a convoy home after the Dieppe raid.

MAJOR GENERAL JOHN ROBERTS
(1891–1962)

John Roberts served as an artilleryman in the First World War, during which he was awarded the Military Cross. Known as "Ham" from his middle name, Hamilton, he was the commander of the Canadian 1st Field Regiment in the Battle of France in 1940 and succeeded in bringing back his artillery during the evacuation from Brest, which won him the reputation as an effective officer. He then commanded the Canadian 2nd Division in a series of field exercises in 1942 in which the division emerged as one of the top four units in the army. As a result, the division was chosen for the Dieppe operation, but failure there, and further failures in major exercises in spring 1943 in preparation for D-Day, led him to be demoted to commanding reinforcement units.

19 AUGUST–19 NOVEMBER 1942

THE BATTLE FOR STALINGRAD

When German and Romanian forces finally reached the outskirts of Stalingrad in mid-August and forced a small salient as far as the Volga river in the north, there was wide confidence at Hitler's headquarters that the city would be in German hands in a matter of days; weeks at the most. On 19 August, Paulus launched a major offensive against the city together with some units of the 4th Panzer Army. On 23 August, the German air force in southern Russia, commanded by General (later Field Marshal) Wolfram von Richthofen, sent 600 bombers to devastate the city. The decision to leave the population in place to avoid the disruption that would be caused by a stream of refugees resulted, according to Soviet estimates, in the death of 40,000 people. The savage bombardment from artillery and aircraft pushed the Soviet defenders back towards the river.

O n 7 September, Paulus massed his forces for a concerted push to drive the Soviet defenders across the Volga. The two armies defending the area, 62nd and 64th, were split apart and block by block, factory by factory, German forces pressed forward. The commander of the 62nd, General Lopatin, thought the situation was hopeless and argued for withdrawal. He was dismissed and his place taken by a young, ebullient commander, Vasily Chuikov. He arrived the same day as the German thrust on 7 September to find a city in ruins. The Red Army survived only by using the destroyed urban landscape as a natural defence. In cellars and warehouses small groups of soldiers hid themselves, sniping at German infiltrators, using the cover of night to retake buildings that had been abandoned to heavier German daytime firepower. During September and October, the German army pushed the 62nd back into a handful of factory complexes – the Red October factory, the Barricades factory – right on the edge of the river.

Neither Paulus nor Chuikov fought a campaign entirely isolated from the rest of the Axis and Soviet forces. A stream of supplies and reinforcements crossed the Volga from the far bank; artillery and rocket fire was directed at German strongholds from the same area. On either flank of the city were much larger Soviet armies: to the south General Yeremenko's Stalingrad Army Group, and to the north the Don Army Group of General Rokossovsky. They provided what assistance they could by attacking the exposed flanks of the German armies, while overhead large numbers of Soviet aircraft, directed in a co-ordinated way by radio (the earliest Soviet example of this), began to contest

OPPOSITE German soldiers storm part of the Red October plant near the edge of the Volga River in the heart of Stalingrad. Each building was fought for room by room.

GENERAL VASILY CHUIKOV
(1900–82)

Chuikov was the son of a peasant family who joined the Red Army during the Russian Civil War. He became a career officer and in 1939 commanded the Soviet 4th Army in the occupation of Poland. His poor performance in the Soviet-Finnish war led to his demotion and he was sent as adviser to Chiang Kaishek in China. He was recalled in May 1942 and posted a few weeks later to command the 64th Army trying to hold the steppe in front of Stalingrad. In September he was transferred to command of the 62nd Army in the defence of the city itself, and distinguished himself as an inspiring, brave and innovative commander. He later commanded the army that reached the centre of Berlin first, in May 1945. In 1955, he was promoted to marshal and was commander-in-chief of the Soviet army from 1960 to 1964. He was buried in Stalingrad on the hill of Mamayev Kurgan, scene of the most bitter fighting in the city.

26 AUGUST 1942

General Zhukov appointed deputy supreme commander-in-chief under Stalin.

12 SEPTEMBER 1942

British liner *Laconia* sunk in the South Atlantic with 1,500 Italian POWs on board.

3 OCTOBER 1942

German rocket scientists successfully launch the A4 missile which was to become the V2 rocket.

4 NOVEMBER 1942

Axis forces in Egypt under Rommel are forced to retreat after defeat in the Second Battle of Alamein.

8 NOVEMBER 1942

Allied forces land in northwest Africa in Operation "Torch".

10 NOVEMBER 1942

German forces occupy Corsica and over the next couple of weeks occupy Vichy France in reaction to the Allied landings in North Africa.

local air superiority for almost the first time in the campaign. German forces were stretched out across the Don Steppe, with the vulnerable corridor into Stalingrad guarded by Hungarian, Italian and Romanian allies. The German 4th Air Fleet was pressed heavily by the battle, but continued to provide assistance to the ground war as well as challenging Soviet air power.

The determination of the 62nd Army to hold the city at all costs has sometimes been attributed to fear of Soviet security forces in the rear who would shoot deserters or defeatists, or send them off to penal battalions. A figure of 13,500 has been estimated for those shot by their own side. But Soviet records show only 203 arrests for "panic" from November 1942 to February 1943 among all the Soviet armies defending Stalingrad. The evidence from eye-witnesses suggests instead that the Soviet defenders had at last found a cause they could identify with and a military challenge that made sense. The Russian novelist Viktor Nekrasov, who served as a junior officer at Stalingrad, found that the battle produced "wonderfully hardened soldiers". German soldiers also fought with great tenacity and desperation. The urban battlefield became a small, enclosed, violent microcosm of the larger battle that surrounded it.

On 9 November, German forces finally succeeded in punching a 500-metre (550-yard) hole in Chuikov's front, reaching the Volga. Soviet troops could not dislodge them, but German exhaustion brought a lull on 12 November. Six days later, Chuikov received a cryptic message from front headquarters that he should stand by for special orders. On the morning of 19 November, Chuikov was told that a massive Soviet counter-offensive had just been launched whose purpose was to cut off and encircle Paulus's 6th Army.

FIELD MARSHAL FRIEDRICH PAULUS
(1890–1957)

Friedrich Paulus was unusual among top German officers in coming from a bourgeois background, though he is often mistakenly described as "von Paulus". The son of a schoolmaster, he served in the German army continuously from 1910. In the 1930s his reputation as a very effective staff officer brought him rapid promotion. By 1939 he was chief-of-staff of the German 10th Army, which was renamed 6th Army for the campaign in Belgium and France. He played a major part in preparing the staff plans for Operation "Barbarossa", and took over command of the 6th Army in January 1942 following the sudden death of Field Marshal Walter von Reichenau. He  was captured at Stalingrad and became a major figure in the Soviet-sponsored National Committee Free Germany, made up of German POWs. After the war he returned to East Germany, where he worked as an inspector of police.

Under "rolling cover" from storm artillery
forces, German infantry enter the suburbs
of Stalingrad, 12 November 1942.

German artillerymen give close support to the infantry as they
edge forward through the ruins of Stalingrad. The picture is from
November 1942, shortly before the encirclement of the 6th Army.

23 OCTOBER–11 NOVEMBER 1942

SECOND ALAMEIN

The Second Battle of El Alamein was the first major victory of British Commonwealth forces against the German enemy and it opened the way to the destruction of Axis forces throughout North Africa. Although the battle was dwarfed by the campaigns on the Eastern Front, it was nonetheless a decisive turning point in Allied fortunes, making the Middle East secure and opening the way for a campaign to liberate the Mediterranean from the Axis.

Rommel knew after the failure at Alam Halfa that he lacked the depth of resources needed to penetrate further into Egypt. Instead, he established a thick defensive line, providing German troops and tanks to strengthen the Italian divisions; the greatest concentration of Axis forces was in the north, protecting communications along the coast. Rommel had four German and a maximum of eight Italian divisions at his disposal (a balance reflected in the decision to rename Panzer Army Africa the German-Italian Panzer Army). The Axis fielded around 500 tanks, of which fewer than half were German, and had support from 350 aircraft. All Axis forces were short of fuel and spare parts. Montgomery, on the other hand, saw his forces grow steadily during September and October. The armoured divisions could call on 1,030 tanks, 300 of which were new American Grants, and there were over 1,500 aircraft in the Middle East and Malta. He refused to act until he was confident that his forces had a decisive superiority and the army understood the nature of his plan.

After years of rapid mobile warfare, the Second Alamein battle was a set-piece operation. Montgomery planned to attack where Rommel was strongest in the north, around Kidney Hill, but to disguise the weight of his assault by diversionary attacks in the south. His object, in what was codenamed Operation "Lightfoot", was to send forward the infantry divisions to open up a pathway through the minefields, and then to pour the tanks of the 10th Armoured Corps through the gap. With a salient secured, a second operation, "Supercharge", would push through large armoured forces for the final blow. The start was set for 23 October, when fortuitously Rommel was away on sick leave.

Operation "Lightfoot" began with a massive artillery barrage in the evening of 23 October. Rommel's replacement, Lieutenant General Stumme, died during the Allied air attacks, leaving Axis forces in some confusion until Rommel's return on 25 October. Nevertheless, resistance was fierce, and only by the second day was progress made along the coast road and around Kidney Hill. Rommel ordered his

FIELD MARSHAL BERNARD MONTGOMERY (1887–1976)

The son of an Anglo-Irish clergyman, Montgomery joined the army in 1908 and saw service in the early battles of the First World War before a bullet in the lung almost killed him. He returned to duty as a staff officer, and served between the wars in Ireland, India, Egypt and Palestine, where he was responsible for suppressing a revolt in 1938. He made his reputation as an excellent trainer of men and a master of meticulous preparation. In the Battle of France he commanded the 3rd Division, which he successfully withdrew at Dunkirk with relatively low casualties. In December 1941 he was appointed Commander-in-Chief Southeastern Command, where he insisted on intensive training for his men. Appointed to command the 8th Army in August 1942, he transformed its morale in a matter of weeks. El Alamein was his most famous victory, and later campaigns in Sicily, Italy and northwest Europe made him a household name. He was a difficult personality – acerbic, intolerant, boastful, egotistical – and this soured his strategic performance. He collaborated poorly with others; tact was entirely foreign to him. He was ground commander for the Normandy invasion, then commander of the 21st Army Group. After the war, he was appointed chief of the Imperial General Staff and created Viscount Montgomery of Alamein.

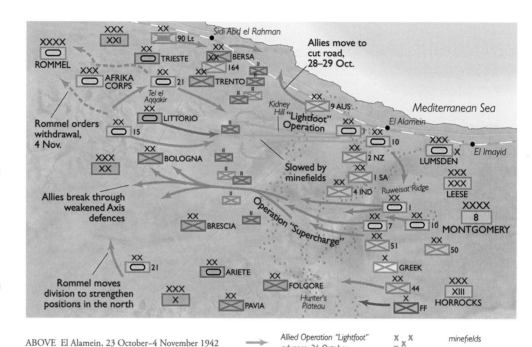

ABOVE El Alamein, 23 October–4 November 1942

⟶ Allied Operation "Lightfoot"
advance, 26 October

⟶ Allied Operation "Supercharge"
advance, 2 November

x x
x x   minefields

13 AUGUST 1942
Montgomery takes over as commander of the 8th Army.

14 OCTOBER 1942
German forces begin major assault on Stalingrad defences to drive Red Army into the Volga.

31 OCTOBER 1942
Heavy German bombing raid on the English cathedral city of Canterbury.

tanks north to dislodge the enemy, but exposed the Italian divisions to Allied attacks, which were pressed forward during fierce armoured fighting on 27 and 28 October. Montgomery then withdrew the diversionary forces in the south and concentrated a heavy armoured force to carry out "Supercharge". When the fresh armour poured through on 2 November, supported by strong air attacks, Rommel realized he was defeated; Axis forces were down to only 35 fully serviceable tanks. Hitler refused permission to withdraw, but two days later he had to accept reality, and Rommel began a rapid westwards retreat along the coast road. Some Italian divisions continued to fight after the German forces had abandoned the battle, but the Axis position was hopeless. Rommel left over 400 destroyed tanks; the Allies lost around 250. Allied casualties were 13,500, but Montgomery's forces netted over 30,000 Axis prisoners.

The 8th Army raced in pursuit of the retreating Rommel and by 13 November had retaken Tobruk. Axis forces made a brief defensive attack on Benghazi on 20 November, and stopped at El Aghelia on 23 November and then retreated again on 11 December – the pressure was relentless. Tripoli was occupied on 23 January and Rommel raced for the last defensive line in Tunisia, the Mareth Line, where Axis forces finally halted and turned. Victory at Alamein was complete and permission was given for church bells in Britain to ring out in celebration for the first time since May 1940.

MARSHAL UGO CAVALLERO
(1880–1943)

A member of the Piedmontese nobility, Cavallero joined the Italian army in 1898 and rose rapidly on account of his organizational and tactical skills. He fought in the Italo-Turkish war of September 1911–October 1912, and during the First World War joined the Italian Supreme Command where he rose to be chief of operations responsible for organizing the Italian victory at Vittorio Veneto. He was a keen fascist and served as undersecretary of war during 1925–28. He left the army, but was recalled in 1937 and took command of Italian forces in East Africa the following year. In December 1940, he succeeded Badoglio as chief of the Italian Supreme Command, and took personal control of the Italian forces in Greece, where he stabilized the front line. He was nominally Rommel's superior for the Axis campaigns in North Africa, but found it difficult to overrule his German allies. He opposed Rommel's invasion of Egypt, and when Libya was lost following Alamein, he was sacked. He committed suicide in September 1943 after refusing Hitler's request to lead those Italian forces still committed to fighting the Allies.

SECOND BATTLE OF ALAMEIN

Diary of Bombadier Leslie Coleman of the 14th Light Anti-Aircraft Regiment, New Zealand Expeditionary Force, 25 October to 12 November 1942. The entries cover the key period of the Second Battle of Alamein and the long Axis retreat.

OCTOBER

25   Sunday

Moved up very close to Jerry dug a pit and settled down to wait events, these were not long in coming, we were soon amidst a barrage of shells and mortars, some were unpleasantly close but did no damage. Very few planes about.

26   .   Monday

Ah! quite good news, we are moving back to our former positions, out of shell fire range.
A bit of bombing going on while on our way back A Stukear raid sual on dusk, bombs rather close to our gun, fire a good few rounds.

OCTOBER

tuasday   27

Morning has been very quiet except for some shelling and bombing raids fire a few shots away at some M.E. 109s.
One of my cobbers killed today with a stray shell. George Price. Moving tonight in behind the Aussies.

Wednesday Moved last 28 night and are now in a beautiful spot our gun is ten yds from the sea. have. spent a lot of time swimming today. first time for some weeks Saw 126 of our bombers go over jerry in 1½ hrs today A big do suppose to be on tonight.

OCTOBER

29   Thursday

Things seemed to go according to plan last night so we have advanced a bit more. Have had two goes at jerries planes today some very close.
Did a fair bit of swimming today, this spot will do me for a week or two. Just had to take posts. Stukas.

30   Friday

Had a very easy day just swimming and spotting for aircraft.
Never fired a shot today, everything out of range for us.
The aim is just swarming with our own planes Also received one bottle of beer
Moving tonight.

OCTOBER

Saturday We moved this morning into positions taken from jerry. a sticky sort of a spot A terrible lot of shells landing round us at present. Just Arrived for a Stukas raid. Could not get our gun into action, because of a bent pin. Very annoyed. Dug a gun pit 3 Stukas raids.

130

1 A great start Sunday
this morning our fighters
intercepted a Stukas raid
shooting down a large
number of them. We had
a few shots at an M.E.
A lot of Artillery
fire going on today

2 Monday
Saw Mr. Parkes this
morning. Have had a
few raids today. We
advanced this morning
2½ miles, into a very
nasty spot. too many
shells landing around
us. Also some Tank
shells. Dug a deep
gun pit, took till dark

---

5 Travelled all Thursday
last night without contacting
Jerry. He seems to be
running very fast. Stopped
for breakfast. Saw two Itis
on a motorbike trying to
get away. Travelled all day
were bombed once by two
M.E. but did not shoot.
Ran into some Artillery
fire, from a pocket of Jerries

Did not go far last Friday
night, had a good nights rest
except when a plane dropped
flares over us. Moved off
in the morning in pouring rain.
Rained most of the day.
Made the coast road between
Mersa & Bargush at dark.
had Tea then moved off up
the hill again. where
we ran into trouble.

Travelled all day Monday
today passing smashed
up jerry stuff all the
way have now reached
Charing Cross. Smashed
Tanks, Planes, trucks of
Jerries are lying everywhere
The slaughter has been
fearful. Have parked up
for the night, just past
Charing Cross.

Moved early this Tuesday
morning and are now getting
quite close to Sidi Barrani.
Travelled all day and
camped on the side of
the road seven miles from
Sidi Barrani. and about
a mile from the sea.
Our gun in good A.A.
position on top of hill

Tuesday **3**
Have spent most of the
day in our holes day
very hot. A Stukas
raid this afternoon
but did not do any
damage. Position on the
close side far out. getting
good rations now.
A big do on tonight.
Artillery fire everywhere.

Wednesday Ah! at last we
have Hermien on the
run and he is running
we are after him
flat out a lot of
prisoners coming in.
We will be travelling
all night tonight so will
get very little sleep
Infact we wont get any
sleep. Smashed trucks
everywhere.

Saturday **7**
What a night, pitch black and
trucks bogged everywhere
shooting flares up to see what
was going on. Our truck &
gun hopelessly bogged spent
a very uncomfortable night
wet through and cold.
This morning we were able
to get onto dry ground
where we stayed all
day trying to get our
Sunday Things day
Things are much better
this morning fine day with
a good drying wind maybe
moving soon.
Yes we have moved
now travelled through
one of Jerries airdromes
smashed planes every-
where he sure had
to move in a hurry.

Wednesday **11** A very rude awaking
this morning Stukas & M.E.
attacked Abandoned airdrome.
Three planes shot down. One
credited to A.A. fire. A lot
of trouble with our gun.
All day in this position. went
for a swim this afternoon. heard
that a sniper had been captured
in the morning. Our gun is now
back to firing order.

Thursday Spent a good Night
Moved this morning. passed
Barani, a tremendous amount of
transport on the road we
stopped to get a new steering block
for our truck. caught the rest
of the convoy up just at lunch
time. Moved on after lunch.
through miles of transport. arrived at
Sollam. Boys found a lot of loot
rifles, flags. etc. very thrilled

131

8 NOVEMBER 1942–14 FEBRUARY 1943

OPERATION "TORCH"

In the summer of 1942 the British and American chiefs-of-staff discussed the possibility of opening a "second front" in France in 1942. A frontal assault was rejected as too risky with unproven American forces and shortages of shipping, and on 22 July it was agreed to launch a smaller combined-arms assault on French North Africa. The object was to help the British in the east to clear the Axis out of Libya and to give American forces an opportunity to gain combat experience. The operation, codenamed "Torch", was to be largely an American affair and it was placed under the command of the recently arrived Lieutenant General Eisenhower.

The plan was to land substantial forces in French Morocco, and at Oran and Algiers in Algeria. It was hoped that the large French garrisons could be persuaded not to oppose the landings, and on 22 October Eisenhower's deputy, Major General Mark Clark, landed secretly in Algeria to make contact with the local commander of French forces, but a guarantee could not be secured that there would be no resistance. The task force sailed in two large formations. The men and equipment for the Moroccan landings under Major General George Patton sailed directly across the Atlantic. A vast armada of 650 warships took the forces for the central and eastern sectors from British ports. The total assault force of 65,000 men was roughly half the size of the French garrison, but was strongly supported by naval vessels and by two large air forces, one for the western landings, one for the east.

The landings on 8 November achieved complete surprise since the fleet was disguised as a convoy bound for Malta. There was strong resistance in Morocco and also in Oran, but in Algiers the situation was confused by a coup launched by 400 French resistance fighters on the day of the landings which immobilized some of the troops and brought the occupation of most government buildings. Vichy forces fought back and tried to resist the Allied landing, but Admiral Darlan, overall commander-in-chief of Vichy French forces, who happened to be in Algiers, finally agreed to a ceasefire, and then promptly tried to withdraw it when the Vichy government refused to endorse his decision. Arrested by the American authorities, he agreed on 10 November to order a ceasefire in Oran, and the following day gave orders for an end to hostilities in Morocco.

The response to the Allied landings was immediate: on 10 November, Hitler ordered the German occupation of Vichy-controlled France; Italian forces occupied Corsica; and Vichy was compelled to agree to the transfer of Axis forces in large numbers to the as yet unoccupied French territory of Tunisia. Darlan tried to persuade the French fleet to sail to North Africa and join the Allies, but the naval command refused and on 27 November the fleet was scuttled at Toulon. When Darlan was murdered on 24 December, his

12–15 NOVEMBER 1942
Battles of Ironbottom Sound in the Solomons result in heavy losses for Japanese convoys to Guadalcanal.

27 NOVEMBER 1942
French fleet scuttled at Toulon.

1 DECEMBER 1942
United States introduces mandatory petrol rationing. across all states.

11 JANUARY 1943
The Chinese Nationalist government makes a formal alliance with Britain and the United States.

14–24 JANUARY 1943
Casablanca Conference where Churchill and Roosevelt decide on future strategy and launch the Combined Bomber Offensive.

23 JANUARY 1943
British Commonwealth forces enter Tripoli.

2 FEBRUARY 1943
German forces surrender in Stalingrad at the end of Operation "Ring".

8 FEBRUARY 1943
Japanese complete evacuation from Guadalcanal.

place was taken by the pro-Allied General Giraud, and French forces willing to fight with the Allies were placed under the field command of General Juin.

The landings were supposed to clear the way to link up with Montgomery's now advancing 8th Army in Libya, but in the race to reach Tunisia the German and Italian forces acted faster, bringing 17,000 troops and substantial numbers of aircraft into the area around Tunis by the end of November. In the south, Rommel reached the defensive Mareth Line and almost the whole of Tunisia was in Axis hands. A combined British and American 1st Army tried to reach Tunis and came within 20 kilometres (32 miles) of their target, but the newly created 5th Panzer Army under General von Arnim succeeded in preventing the breakthrough and the 1st Army ground to a halt in poor weather and deep mud. During January 1943, the Axis forces succeeded in a number of small operations in pushing back French and British forces and stabilizing a defensive line in the Dorsale Mountains. By early February, with Rommel's forces arrived in Tunisia, a formidable garrison had been formed. An operation that had promised a quick end to the Axis presence in North Africa had instead provoked a final stand.

American troops of the Centre Task Force disembark a landing craft on their way towards the beaches near the Algerian port of Oran.

GENERAL DWIGHT D. EISENHOWER
(1890–1969)

The son of a poor Texas family, Eisenhower succeeded in entering the West Point Military Academy and embarked on a military career that made him one of the United States' most famous generals. He failed to see active service in the First World War – he was recruited to create America's first tank corps – and between the wars held various staff appointments before being posted to the Philippines to serve with MacArthur. In December 1939, he returned to the United States and by the end of September 1941 was a brigadier general and chief-of-staff of the 3rd Army. After Pearl Harbor, General Marshall made him head of the new Operations Division. He was chosen to command the American European Theater of Operations in June 1942, and was supreme commander for the "Torch" landings, having never yet heard a shot fired in anger. He became supreme commander of the invasion of northwest Europe, for which his diplomatic and organizational skills and amiable disposition made him an ideal candidate. After the war, he became United States Army chief-of-staff until 1948, and was president of the United States from 1953 to 1961.

ADMIRAL FRANÇOIS DARLAN
(1881–1942)

Darlan was a successful and ambitious French naval officer, who joined the navy in 1902 and rose by 1936 to the rank of admiral and naval chief-of-staff. In 1939, he was given the unique title of "admiral of the fleet" and put in supreme command of French naval forces. He was a firm supporter of Pétain and in February 1941 became Pétain's deputy and effective head of the government. He collaborated with the German occupiers, and in May 1941 agreed the Paris Protocols that gave substantial concessions to the Germans in French Africa and the Middle East. In April 1942, the Germans, uncertain of Darlan's reliability, pressured Pétain to replace him with Laval. Darlan remained commander-in-chief of French forces. On 7 November he arrived in Algiers to visit his sick son and was caught up in the "Torch" invasions. He changed sides, agreed to a French ceasefire, and was declared high commissioner for French North Africa, but on 24 December he was assassinated by a French royalist resistance fighter, Fernand de la Chapelle, who was executed two days later.

SECRET
C O P Y

WAR DEPARTMENT
Washington, D.C.

September 10, 1942.

My dear General Eisenhower:

A meticulous study of the coastline adjacent to CASABLANCA
confirms the belief I have already expressed to you, that the landings
must take place at three points.

The southernmost of these is SAFI, which is selected because
it is the only secondary port in the entire littoral of Africa within
our purview which permits the docking of two large vessels.

The next point to the north is FEDALA, which is selected
because of its proximity — some 18 miles — to CASABLANCA and owing
to the very unmobile state of amphibious infantry a principal landing
must take place within foot marching distance of the objective.

The third point of landing is RABAT. It is selected because
there are two excellent landing fields — that on the north of the river
being easily accessible from the highway which passes close to the beach
and, further, an attack north of the river obviates the necessity of
street fighting in the town of RABAT, itself.

The beaches at all the places selected are inadequate and
fairly well defended, but they are the best available. However, in
view of this fact, I believe that it is patent that our losses due to
surf conditions may well be excessive and, therefore, that it behooves
us to provide all additional infantry which we can crowd in, even if
that infantry has nothing but its normal infantry weapons and is devoid
of supply vehicles.

In view of the foregoing, we propose to attack at SAFI with
one infantry battalion combat team combat loaded, supported by an infantry
battalion (less equipment). Whether or not this battalion will come
from the 9th Division or from the 41st Infantry, in the 2d Armored Division,
has not been determined. These two battalions will seize the harbor and
permit the unloading at the dock of the two vessels, one AP and one AK,
carrying the light armored combat team. As soon as these vessels are
unloaded they will withdraw and the seatrain, carrying some 200 armored
vehicles accompanied by a transport with personnel to man the vehicles,
will land at the dock and commence unloading. While this is going on,

SECRET

- 1 -

the infantry will hold the beachhead and with the light armored combat team will proceed rapidly on MARRAKECH, with the object of destroying the airfield there and of capturing the town or persuading the Governor, who is pro-American, to surrender.

Simultaneously with this attack, two regimental combat teams of the 3d Division, combat loaded, will force a landing at FEDALA and having secured the harbor will cover the unloading of the second light armored combat team. On the completion of this operation, the entire force will move against CASABLANCA.

The landing at RABAT will be conducted by a regimental combat team of the 3d Division (less one battalion -- this battalion is at SAFI), supported by one light armored combat team, 2d Armored Division. The purpose of this landing is to seize and stock the airfield north of SALI, the native town opposite RABAT, and to capture the outer harbor of RABAT to permit the unloading of the armored combat team. Upon the capture of the airport, the armored combat team will proceed rapidly south to join with the forces landed at FEDALA. The infantry will hold the airport initially captured and if circumstances permit will attack and capture the second airport south of the river and just southeast of the town of RABAT.

If the unloading of the seatrain progresses as rapidly as may be hoped, the 200 armored vehicles which it contains should be able to start moving north at D + 36 to 48 hours. This movement would cut off possible reinforcements and add tremendously to the weight of the attack on CASABLANCA and to the apparent power of the operation. The light armored combat team from MARRAKECH, moving via the MARRAKECH - CASABLANCA road, should also be coming in and, in addition to preventing the arrival of hostile reinforcements, should eventually add its weight to the assault on CASABLANCA.

You will note that in every case we have planned to land the armored units at wharves. If we should be fortunate enough to have calm weather, we could land part of them on the beach, but it is unwise to so plan.

Navy air support of the attack will operate as follows: There will be one converted carrier covering the attack on SAFI. There will be one fleet carrier and one converted carrier covering the attacks on FEDALA and RABAT, with particular attention to the hostile submarines known to be in CASABLANCA. Should our project of securing the CHARGER materialize — and I believe that it will — we will have about 54 Army fighters that will be available when the airport is captured and who will also be available in case of emergency, immediately the attack starts.   By an emergency I mean that if the French fighters and bombers prove too much for the Navy air, we would have to uee our Army fighters at once and trust to capture the airport within two hours.   Failing this, they would have to land in the desert, which they can do with considerable safety.

The second echelon of air to come from UK will be called for by me, through you, as soon as the field at RABAT is in our hands.

I append hereto a list indicating the components of the 1st, 2d and 3d Convoys, with the proposed dates of their arrival.

Sincerely yours,

/s/ G. S. Patton, Jr.

G. S. PATTON, Jr.,
Major General, U. S. Army.

Incl.

Lieut. General Dwight D. Eisenhower,
    Commanding General, European Theater,
        United States Army,
            20 Grosvenor Square,
                London England.

CONVOYS -- TASK FORCE "A"

1st Convoy (Assault) D Day

1 - Task Force Hq (Fwd Ech)
1 - 3d Div Amp (Div Hq (Fwd Ech) and 3 R C T)
1 - Bn CT (9th Div) (Stripped to less than minimum vehicles)
3 - Small Arm'd CT's, 2d Arm'd Div, each consisting of:
      2 Cos Lt Tank, 1 Co Arm'd Inf, 1 Btry FA (4 guns),
      1 Recon Plat, and small Sig, Med, and Maint Secs
1 - Arm'd Combat Command of 200 vehicles (seatrain) built
      around 2 Bns Med Tank, 2d Arm'd Div
1 - Avn Ground Crew, 4,000
2 - Bns AW CA AA (Bofors) stripped to guns
1 - Ground Air Support Command
    Sig Det (RI, Photo, and Sig Serv)
    Engr Det (Top)
    Civil Government and interpreter personnel.

2d Convoy (Personnel and some cargo, lifted in fast cargo ships, D + 5

1 - Engr Regt (Combat)
  - Aviation Ground Crews
2 - Regts CA (AA) (-1 AW Bn)
2 - Bns FA (105 + SP)
1 - Sig Bn (less dets)
1 - Sig Serv Co (less dets)
1 - Sig Photo Co (less dets)
1 - Radio Int Co (less dets)
  - Task Force Hq (less dets)
1 - Port Hq, plus Det Hq, Tpn Corps
2 - Bns QM Port
1 - Bn QM Service
2 - Engr Regts (GS)
1 - Engr Bn (WS)
1 - Engr Co (Top)(Corps)(minus dets)
1 - QM Truck Regt (less 3 Cos)
3 - QM Truck Cos (Sep)
1 - QM Co (GS)
1 - QM Co (Rhd)
4 - Ord Cos (MM)
1 - Bn Ord (Amm)
1 - Ord Co (HM) (FA)
2 - Ord Cos (HM) (Tks)
2 - Ord Cos (Depot)
1 - QM Bn (MM)
2 - Cos Maint Bn (Arm'd Div)
1 - Evac Hosp (Mtz) 400 bed

SECRET

12 NOVEMBER 1942–8 FEBRUARY 1943

GUADALCANAL

The battle for Guadalcanal reached a critical point by November 1942.
Though on a scale very much smaller than the battles in the North African
desert or around Stalingrad, the struggle for the island came to be regarded
by both sides as a vital testing ground for American resolve on the one
hand and Japan's capacity to protect her new-won empire on the other.

A Japanese ship in the major base at Rabaul is hit by a bomb
from the US 5th Army Air Force during an attack. Air attack
on the base neutralized it as a threat throughout the conquest
of the Solomons and the other southwest Pacific islands.

Japanese forces on the island were strengthened after the failure of the
October assault on the American-held Henderson airfield by men
shipped in Japanese naval vessels on the "Tokyo Express" supply route
through the central Solomons. By 12 November the forces at the disposal
of Lieutenant General Hyakutake exceeded American numbers for the
first time – 23,000 against 22,000. But that same day a United States
task force delivered reinforcements to Guadalcanal supported by air
cover from aircraft carriers in the Coral Sea and heavy bombers on the
island of Espiritu Santo. By early December the balance was once again in
American favour, 40,000 troops against 25,000.

This situation might well have been reversed had it not been for a
series of destructive naval battles off the northern coast of Guadalcanal
between 12 and 15 November in which a United States task force
tried to prevent further reinforcement. A large convoy of Japanese
troops, heavily supported by naval vessels, arrived off Guadalcanal in
Ironbottom Sound on the night of 12–13 November. A fierce ship-to-
ship engagement followed which left six American ships sunk and cost
the Japanese three, including a battleship. The following day American
aircraft attacked the Japanese landing fleet, sinking a cruiser and seven
transport ships. During the night of 14–15 November a second major

8 NOVEMBER 1942
US and British forces land in northwest Africa at the start of Operation "Torch".

11 NOVEMBER 1942
The Moroccan city of Casablanca surrenders to the Allies.

20 NOVEMBER 1942
The RAF launches a large-scale bombing attack against the Italian industrial city of Turin.

2 DECEMBER 1942
Scientists working on the top-secret Manhattan Project produce the first nuclear chain reaction.

18 JANUARY 1943
Blockade of Leningrad is broken when a narrow strip of land is opened towards the city, but siege continues.

8 FEBRUARY 1943
The Red Army retakes the city of Kursk, creating a large salient in the German front line in central Russia.

8 FEBRUARY 1943
British 8th Army under Montgomery enters Tunisia for the final showdown with the Axis in North Africa.

RIGHT Tired US soldiers on their way back to Base Operations camp on Guadalcanal, February 1943, after 21 days of continuous combat. The fighting conditions for both sides were exceptionally tough throughout the island campaign.

naval engagement took place in which the Japanese battleship *Kirishima* and a destroyer were sunk for the loss of three US destroyers. In the end only 2,000 troops could be landed, with virtually no military supplies. The battles of Ironbottom Sound marked the end of Japanese efforts to save the position on Guadalcanal. One further attempt was made when Rear Admiral Tanaka personally commanded his destroyer squadron on 30 November in a run to Guadalcanal. His eight destroyers were surprised by a larger American force of five cruisers and four destroyers in Ironbottom Sound, but Tanaka's skilful handling of his ships produced a salvo of torpedoes that sank one cruiser and crippled the remaining three, before Tanaka retreated back up the Slot. The Battle of Tassafaronga, as it was known, was a tactical victory, but no supplies reached the embattled Japanese garrison.

In December 1942 the 1st Marine Division was replaced on the island by the 25th US Infantry Division and Vandegrift was replaced as commander by Major General Alexander Patch, commander of the Americal Division (a contraction of "American New Caledonian"). With more than 50,000 men under his command, he began a series of offensives against the poorly supplied Japanese. By this stage the Japanese navy command had decided that Guadalcanal would have to be abandoned and the Japanese Imperial Headquarters confirmed this decision on 31 December. The isolated Japanese forces fought

REAR ADMIRAL RAIZO TANAKA
(1892–1969)

A career officer in the Japanese navy, Tanaka became an expert on torpedoes in the 1920s and taught at the navy's torpedo school. In September 1941 he was appointed to command Destroyer Squadron 2 and in October promoted to rear admiral. He fought in the invasion of the Philippines and the Dutch East Indies. During the Solomons campaign Tanaka's destroyer force supplied Japanese forces on Guadalcanal along the "Slot" between the islands of the Solomons group. The Japanese called the supply runs "rat transportation", but the Allies nicknamed them the "Tokyo Express". Tanaka became critical of Japanese strategy and was redeployed to shore duties in Burma, where he remained for the rest of the war.

with suicidal determination but were pressed back to the north of the island. Unknown to the Americans, Japanese destroyers off the coast successfully evacuated 10,650 troops, including Hyakutake, between 2 and 8 February, leaving Guadalcanal in American hands.

Japanese losses for the island struggle were high. Over 20,000 troops were lost, 860 aircraft and 15 warships. The United States Navy also lost heavily, but the ground troops suffered only 6,111 casualties, including 1,752 killed. This remarkable disparity in losses was to be repeated in the island battles across the Pacific. If the Battle of Midway had determined the limit of Japanese naval expansion, the failure at Guadalcanal decisively halted the onward march of the Japanese army.

BATTLE FOR NEW GUINEA

While the struggle was continuing in Guadalcanal, a second battle was taking place in eastern New Guinea where the Japanese had landed on 21 July 1942 to try to seize Port Moresby and expel Allied forces from the island. They landed at Gona and Buna and marched inland to seize Kokoda, and by September were 40 kilometres (25 miles) from the port. Stiff Australian and American resistance and the crisis in Guadalcanal forced a Japanese retreat and on 15 November Kokoda was recaptured. On 9 December the Japanese lodgement at Gona was eliminated by the Australian army and on 1 January 1943 Buna was captured as well. Japanese failure in New Guinea was further evidence that the outer perimeter of the southern zone could not be made secure.

Japanese prisoners, sick and hungry, are taken down to the beach by American troops after the capture of a Japanese stronghold on Guadalcanal, 22 February 1943. Most Japanese troops had been evacuated to safety by this time.

Report from Marine First Lieutenant G. S. De Vane on operations in the Solomons in early August 1942 for the capture of the port of Tulagi. The map shows the island of Gavutu, off the southern tip of Malaita and a short distance from Tulagi.

---

17 Aug. 1942

From: Bn. 2 3rd Bn., 2nd Marines

To: Asst. D-2, 1st Marine Division

Subject: Gavutu, Tanambogo operation, Intelligence Report on:

Reference: 1. Verbal order of Asst D-2 dated 17 Aug. 1942.
2. Report of Bn 1 of 3rd Bn, 2nd Marines dated 19 August 1942.

1. The following report upon the operation of this battalion on Gavutu and Tanambogo Islands as submitted in accordance with Reference 1 above.

A. Personnel -

(1) Thirteen (13) Japanese prisoners were captured alive between the dates of 8 Aug. 1942 and 15 Aug. 1942. These prisoners were delivered to Asst. D-2 at Tulagi. This battalion obtained no information from the above-mentioned prisoners because no interpreter was available.

(2) This echelon estimates that 670 Japanese occupied the islands of Gavutu and Tanambogo. The majority of these men apparently were attached to a naval unit because the captured uniforms had anchor insignia sewn on the sleeves and caps. No insignia of rank was found.

(3) A total of about 655 Japanese were buried on the two islands. 155 were buried in the caves and tunnels in the hills on the islands.

(4) A number of Japanese were found who were wearing nothing but a loin cloth and a pair of sneakers or no shoes at all. In numerous cases Japanese swam over from Florida island.

HIST 0966 DIV

---

2)

entirely unarmed.

(5) The patience and persistence of the Japanese soldiers was amazing. Their fearlessness was demonstrated on several occasions when unarmed Japanese would attack armed marines in groups several times the size of Japanese groups. Japanese snipers in cocoanut trees were very harrasing in spite of the fact that their rifle fire was inaccurate at ranges of 100 yards or more. Their mastery of the art of camouflage was shown by the perfect concealment of Japanese snipers in trees and on the beaches under rocks.

B. Captured material.

(1) The standard infantry rifle used on the islands was a .25 caliber rifle. Reports were made that soft nosed or blunt nosed bullets might have been used. It is a bolt action rifle which has a sight that can be elevated but which can not be changed for windage. The metal is very rust-resisting.

(2) Several 13 MM anti aircraft guns were captured. In one emplacement two barrels were on one mount and the trigger was foot operated. One 3 in. dual purpose gun was destroyed on Gavutu and another was still in operation.

(3) The Japanese MGs captured fire a .303 cal. cartridge. It should be noted here that these Japanese machine guns can fire .30 cal. ammunition, but that the .30 cal. BMG can not use .303 ammunition. In several places the butt plates

3/ of the Jap MGs had been disposed of which made the captured MGs unusable.

(4) Two landing barges with twin keels were captured at the Gavutu jetty. The motors are apparently of aluminum, horse power unknown and may use kerosene or gasoline.

(5) Seven torpedoes found on the jetty appear to be of the size used by midget submarines. No other evidence of any submarine activity was found.

(6) A quantity of incendiary and carbide bombs were found at the northern shore of Tanambogo.

(7) A fuel truck, make and model unreported, was reported found near one of the fuel dumps on Florida Island. This was at Halavo.

(8) A small quantity of Diesel fuel was found on Gavutu. About 600 drums of hi-test gasoline were found at the Fla. village across the channel and north of Tanambogo.

C. Installations

(1) The radio station, reported to be 500 watts, on the south end of the hill on Gavutu, was partially destroyed by bombing.

(2) No hospitalization facilities were found. This, coupled with the absence of shore batteries, probably indicates that the Japanese had not completed their defenses, or that an attack was not anticipated.

(3) Four barracks buildings, constructed of corrugated metal were located on the eastern shore of Tanambogo.

(4) What appeared to be an Officer's club or officers quarters, was found on the

4/ northern shore of Gavutu. In the building were a number of large bottles of what was reported to be an intoxicating drink.

(5) Buoys or moorings for seaplanes are indicated on the attached sketch.

(6) Power plants were found on both Gavutu and Tanambogo. A line, probably a power line, connected Gaomi to Tanambogo Island.

(7) Several jetties have been reported to have been found on the adjoining shores of Florida Island. Their proximity to the fuel dumps there indicates that they were used in connection with fueling planes.

(8) The seaplane ramps, workshops, and other seaplane facilities were located mainly on Tanambogo. However, the attached sketch indicates that the seaplane buoys or moorings also were in the Gavutu area. Aviation gas was found both on Gavutu and Tanambogo.

D. The three (3) Japanese planes destroyed by naval gunfire or by bombing, the seaplane ramps, the aviation gasoline, workshop facilities, and the bombs —— all this seems to indicate that the Gavutu - Tanambogo - Gaomi Islands area was used extensively as a base for seaplanes.

The jetty on the shore of Gavutu as indicated on the accompanying sketch, is of concrete and wood pilings. Alongside the jetty the water appears to be about fifteen feet deep. On the jetty itself is a marine railway. Fuel dumps were very near the jetty, and on the jetty itself were a number of large tanks, a workshop, and the seven torpedoes previously mentioned.

F. All documents, maps, blueprints, the fighter aircraft sight, weapons, ammunition and the other information and material have been turned over to the Asst. Division Commander at Tulagi. Reference 2 is a list of all quartermaster property which has been delivered to assistant D.+ at Tulagi.

G. S. DeVane, 1st Lt.
BN 2, 3rd Bn. 2nd Mar.

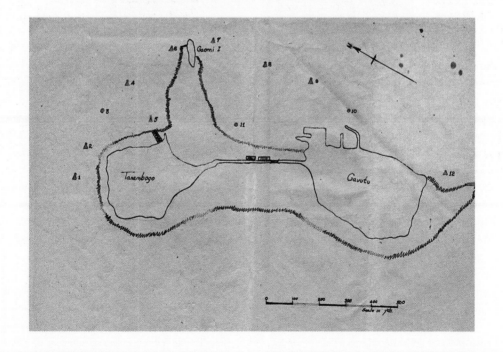

DEFEAT AT STALINGRAD

The success of the Soviet Operation "Uranus" sealed the fate of an estimated 200–250,000 Axis troops in the Stalingrad pocket, including the 6th Army, most of the 4th Panzer Army and some units from Germany's Axis allies. Though there were stocks of ammunition and food in the city and three working airfields, supply to the trapped force failed to materialize on the scale promised. The airlift averaged less than 100 tons a day and the German air force lost 488 transport aircraft in the process. By January, food rations were down to 55 grams (two ounces) of bread a day and 28 grams (an ounce) of sugar. It was possible to fly out around 30,000 wounded men, but thousands of others suffering from frostbite and dysentery fought on from fear of what might happen to them or in the hope that rescue might be possible.

The Soviet High Command believed that the city contained only 80,000 of the enemy and that their exposed position would lead them to surrender. A force of 47 Soviet divisions was drawn up around the Stalingrad area, with 300 aircraft and 179 tanks to fulfil what was codenamed Operation "Kol'tso" (Ring). The attack was scheduled for 10 January, but Paulus was given the opportunity to surrender two days before, which he refused out of hand. Soviet planners expected the operation to last only a few days, but their miscalculation of the size of the trapped force resulted in a campaign of three weeks before the battle was over.

Operation "Kol'tso" began with the largest artillery barrage the Red Army had yet mounted. Paulus's forces were stretched out in open country around Stalingrad as well as in the ruins of the city. The steppe was quickly cleared, reducing the pocket to half its original size within a week. But the Soviet forces found fighting amidst the urban ruins as difficult as the Germans' experience of it. In the heart of the city General Chuikov's 62nd Army was still fighting its own battle, turned now from defender into attacker by the success of the encirclement. His army pushed German troops back from the riverfront block by block. On 22 January, Soviet armies grouped for a final push into the city. Isolating each quarter at a time, they eliminated remaining resistance. German soldiers began to surrender in large numbers. On 26 January, contact was finally made between Chuikov's army and the vanguard of the attacking force near the Barricades Factory. By 31 January, Heroes of the Revolution Square, in the centre of the city, was finally reached.

Interrogators discovered that Paulus was sheltering in the Univermag department store on one side of the square. A young Soviet officer, Lieutenant Fyodor Yelchenko, was led into the basement of the building, where he found an unkempt and miserable commander. Paulus agreed

10 NOVEMBER 1942
Admiral Darlan agrees to a general ceasefire in North Africa following "Torch" invasion.

2 JANUARY 1943
Allied forces capture the New Guinea port of Buna.

13 JANUARY 1943
Hitler issues his so-called "Total War" decree, calling for the highest sacrifices from the German people.

to surrender and was taken away by car to Rokossovsky's headquarters. In the north of the city, the remnants of the 4th Panzer Army fought a fierce final action, but were finally forced to surrender on 2 February. The defeat was the worst ever suffered by the German army. Some 91,000 went into captivity, but an estimated 147,000 had died in combat, or of frostbite, disease and hunger during the course of the battle. Soviet losses for the operations to encircle and destroy the Stalingrad pocket numbered 485,000, including 155,000 dead or captured.

Stalingrad was a signal that the tide had finally turned in the German-Soviet war. Most of the German army was still deep in the Soviet Union, stretched out along a 2,400-kilometre (1,500-mile front), but the contest between the two sides was no longer one-way. The victory reversed the long period of demoralization and uncertainty among Soviet leaders and the wider public. Stalin got himself appointed Marshal of the Soviet Union, his first military title. In Germany the defeat was greeted with disbelief and anxiety. Hitler, who had promoted Paulus to field marshal the day before the capitulation, was outraged that Paulus had not committed suicide. The day following German surrender, the radio repeatedly played "Siegfried's Funeral March" from Wagner's *Twilight of the Gods*.

VICTORY STATUE, VOLGOGRAD

In 1967 the remarkable statue "The Motherland Calls" was officially dedicated in a ceremony on the Mamayev Kurgan hill in the centre of Volgograd (formerly Stalingrad). Sometimes known as "Mother Motherland" or "The Motherland", the colossal statue was the tallest sculpture in the world, 85 metres (279 feet) high, with a vast sword some 33 metres (108 feet) long, and weighing 7,900 tons. From the foot of the hill 200 steps lead up to the monument, one for each day of the siege of Stalingrad. The principal sculptor was Yevgeny Vuchetich and the chief engineer was Nikolai Nikitin. The model for the statue was a native of Stalingrad, Valentina Izotova. The site was a symbolic recognition of the historic turning point in the war with Germany represented by the Battle of Stalingrad.

MARSHAL ALEXANDER NOVIKOV
(1900–76)

A career infantry officer from 1919, Novikov switched to the air force in 1933 as a very young chief of operations, but fell foul of the purges in 1937, when he was expelled from the armed forces. Reinstated, by 1939 he was chief-of-staff of the air force in the Leningrad Military District and a year later promoted to major general. A talented and creative military thinker, in April 1942 he was appointed commander-in-chief of the Soviet air force. He organized air forces into independent air divisions and corps and improved air-ground co-ordination. His forces played an important part in eliminating the Stalingrad pocket, destroying around 1,200 German aircraft. After the war, he began to plan the postwar Soviet air force, but in April 1946 he was arrested, tortured into confessing absurd crimes and sent to a Gulag camp for 15 years. He was released in 1953 on Stalin's death and reinstated. He retired in 1958 to head the Civil Aviation School.

ABOVE German soldiers unloading a Heinkel He 111 inside the Stalingrad "cauldron". The only way they could be supplied was by air and by late January there was just one working airfield left, bringing in supplies and taking out the wounded and the mail.

This proclamation was issued and signed by Adolf Hitler on 26 November 1942 to the troops of the German 6th Army and 4th Panzer Army trapped in the pocket at Stalingrad. Hitler promised to do everything in his power to help his forces in their "heroic struggle" but by 2 February 1943 all German resistance ended. (See translation, page 157.)

The wreckage of a German unit in the battle for Stalingrad. The dead lay where they had fallen, left rigid by the extreme cold.

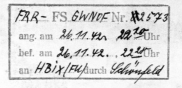

FRR – FS.GWNOF Nr. N2573
ang. am 26.11.42. 22²⁰ Uhr
bef. am 26.11.42. 22²⁵ Uhr
an HBix/FU durch Schönfeld

26. 11. 1942.

Soldaten der 6. Armee und der 4.Panzer-Armee !

Der Kampf um S t a l i n g r a d geht seinem Höhepunkt entgegen.

Der Feind ist im Rücken der deutschen Truppen durchgebrochen und versucht nunmehr verzweifelt, dieses für ihn ausschlaggebende Bollwerk an der Wolga wieder in seinen Besitz zu bringen.

Mit mir sind in diesen schweren Stunden die Gedanken des ganzen deutschen Volkes bei Euch !

Jhr müsst die unter der Führung tatkräftiger Generale mit soviel Blut eroberte Position Stalingrad unter allen Umständen halten !

Es muss unser unabänderlicher Entschluss sein: dass, so wie im Frühjahr bei Charkow, auch dieser Durchbruch des Russen am Ende durch die eingeleiteten

14 FEBRUARY–13 MAY 1943

THE END OF THE AXIS
IN AFRICA: TUNISIA

After the success of the Second Battle of Alamein and the "Torch" landings in North Africa, the Allies had hoped to complete the elimination of enemy resistance within weeks. Instead Rommel successfully brought his battered Afrika Korps back to southern Tunisia by the end of January 1943, while in the north the 5th Panzer Army and the remnants of the Italian 1st Army, despite shortages of equipment, oil and ammunition, established a new Axis front line running the whole length of Tunisia.

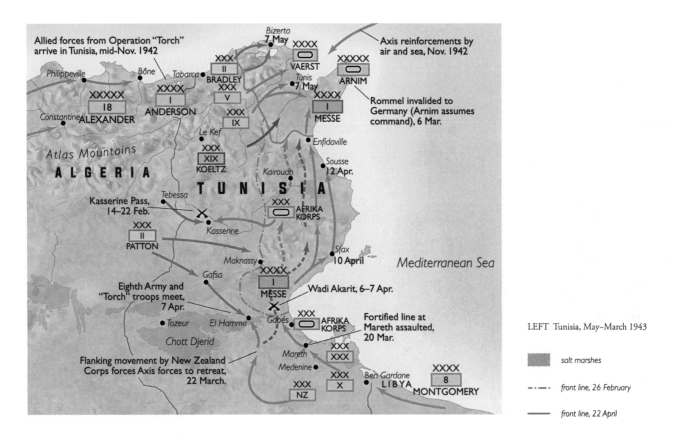

LEFT Tunisia, May–March 1943

salt marshes

– · – · – front line, 26 February

———— front line, 22 April

The Allied plan was to try to divide the northern force under General von Arnim from Rommel's forces in the south with a drive by the US 1st Armored Division to the coastal port of Sfax (Operation "Satin"). But shortages of supply led to the cancellation of "Satin", and instead von Arnim and then Rommel took the initiative in attacking the US 2nd Corps from the eastern Dorsale Mountains in central Tunisia. On 14 February, the American force was driven back to the Kasserine Pass, and there, on 20 February, Rommel – some of whose forces had moved up from the southern Mareth Line – inflicted a heavy defeat on the retreating American army. German units pushed on beyond the pass, but by 22 February they were halted by British and American counter-attacks. Rommel moved back through the mountains, and moved south to defend against an anticipated attack by Montgomery's 8th Army.

The baptism of fire for American forces against experienced German and Italian troops was a harsh one. Relations between the American, British and French forces were strained and supplies were difficult to bring across the long North African routes in poor weather and mud. Eisenhower appointed General Alexander to restore order to the Allied front and complete the destruction of the Axis pocket. Much depended on Montgomery breaching the Mareth Line, but in early March Rommel

6 MARCH 1943

Stalin is named marshal of the Soviet Union and aquires a handsome new uniform.

13 APRIL 1943

Germans reveal the Katyn massacres of Polish officers by the Soviet security service, carried out in 1940.

17 APRIL 1943

Allies set up a planning centre in London under General Morgan to prepare the invasion of Europe in 1944.

18 APRIL 1943

Japanese Admiral Yamamoto, commander of the Japanese navy, is shot down and killed by US fighter aircraft on a flight over the Solomons.

Local inhabitants in Tunis leave the city during the spring of 1943 to avoid the final showdown between Allied and Axis forces which reached its peak in May.

launched his own offensive. On 6 March, three Panzer divisions moved forward, but Montgomery, warned in advance by decrypted German messages, had prepared a trap. Rommel's tanks ran into a wall of withering anti-tank fire and were forced to retreat. On 9 March, Rommel flew to see Hitler to demand more assistance, but instead he was ordered on sick leave, his command taken by von Arnim.

On 20–21 March, Montgomery attacked with the bulk of the 8th Army against the Mareth defences, while the New Zealand Division was sent in a wide outflanking movement through hilly country to capture El Hamma in the Axis rear. Poor weather made progress slow in the frontal assault, and further armour was sent on the flanking attack. To the north, Alexander ordered the US 2nd Corps to drive for the coast and cut off the Axis retreat. The assault proved too difficult, and when Axis forces were compelled in late March to abandon the Mareth Line, they moved northwards, pursued by the 8th Army until they met up with the remaining German and Italian forces in the north of the country. On 7 April, 8th Army troops met up with American forces coming from the northwest.

COLONEL GENERAL HANS-JÜRGEN VON ARNIM
(1889–1962)

The son of a Prussian general, von Arnim joined the German army in 1907, fought in the First World War on the Western and Eastern fronts, and in the 1920s became commander of the elite 68th Infantry Regiment. He commanded divisions in Poland and France, and commanded the 17th Panzer Division for the invasion of the Soviet Union. He was seriously wounded a few days into the campaign, but by November 1942 had risen to command a Panzer corps. He was sent to North Africa to command the 5th Panzer Army and promoted to colonel general. When Rommel was invalided in March, he took over command of the Afrika Korps. He was captured by Indian troops in May 1943 and asked to be taken to Eisenhower. The Allied commander refused to meet any senior German officer until final surrender. Von Arnim was released in 1947.

BELOW An American M3 Lee tank patrolling the streets of the Tunisian port of Bizerta, 8 May 1943. The city had fallen to the US II Corps the day before.

MARSHAL GIOVANNI MESSE
(1883–1968)

Marshal Messe was generally regarded as one of the most successful of Italian commanders in the Second World War. He joined the army in 1901, served in the Italo-Turkish war in 1911–12, and fought in the First World War, during which he was decorated for exceptional bravery and promoted to lieutenant colonel. He saw service in the Ethiopian war as a deputy divisional commander and in 1936 was promoted to general in command of the 3rd Mobile Division. He saw service in Albania in 1939 and in the Italian-Greek war in 1940–41. In July 1941, he was appointed commander of the Italian expeditionary force for the Eastern Front and fought in the battles on the Don towards Stalingrad, but was sent back to Italy in November 1942 for questioning Italian strategy. In February, he was sent to command Italian forces in Tunisia. He was promoted to Marshal of Italy on 12 May, and surrendered the following day. After the Italian surrender in September 1943, Messe was freed and returned to Italy to become chief of the Italian General Staff on the Allied side.

Von Arnim and the Italian commander, Marshal Messe, organized a final stand in the northeast corner of the country around Bizerta and Tunis. They judged their position to be hopeless, but after a meeting between Hitler and Mussolini in Salzburg on 8 April, they were ordered to hold fast at all costs. Supply was down to a fraction of what was needed. In three weeks in April, Allied fighter aircraft destroyed 432 Axis planes for the loss of just 35, including half the entire German air transport fleet. Axis forces had just 150 tanks, against more than 1,500 on the Allied side. Alexander ordered the American 2nd Corps to the north opposite the port of Bizerta; the British 1st Army under Lieutenant General Kenneth Anderson stood opposite Tunis; while the 8th Army occupied the southern section of the Allied noose. On 6 May, a general offensive was launched. Bombarded from the air and artillery, short of almost all essential supplies, Axis resistance collapsed. Bizerta and Tunis fell on 7 May, and five days later von Arnim, who had retreated to the very furthest tip of Tunisia on Cape Bon, surrendered. Marshal Messe, further south, surrendered to Montgomery a day later with the scattered remnants of his 1st Italian Army. Some 240,000 prisoners were taken, a defeat that ranked in numbers with Stalingrad three months before.

A wounded British soldier shares a cigarette with a captured German soldier during the battles for the Mareth Line in southern Tunisia in March 1943. In the end 125,000 Germans were captured in Tunisia.

5–13 JULY 1943

THE BATTLE OF KURSK

After the disaster at Stalingrad it was necessary for the German army in the Soviet Union to win back the initiative. Between 29 January and 23 March, a series of battles took place around the city of Kharkov, the Soviet Union's fourth-largest city, reducing it to rubble in the process. An overstretched Soviet offensive was driven back past Kharkov by the forces of von Manstein's Army Group South (the renamed Army Group Don) as far as the city of Belgorod. This offensive created the southern side of a large Soviet salient, 190 kilometres (120 miles) wide and 95 kilometres (60 miles) long, bulging into the German front line around the city of Kursk. It was here that von Manstein and the army High Command decided the key battle of the summer 1943 campaign should be fought. The operation was codenamed "Zitadelle" (Citadel).

The German plan followed a predictable pattern. The object was to drive two heavily armed wedges into the neck of the salient from north and south to encircle and cut off the large Soviet forces stationed there. Victory here would allow German forces to swing either south again or to move behind Moscow and turn the Soviet line. A force of 900,000 men in 50 divisions, 2,000 aircraft and 2,700 tanks was assembled, including the new heavy Panther and Tiger tanks and the Ferdinand self-propelled gun. Hitler was uncertain about the operation and refused von Manstein's request to begin in May before the Red Army was ready. In the end, he postponed the start date until early July.

The interval gave the Soviet High Command plenty of time to prepare the battlefield. Zhukov and the General Staff guessed the German plan

Soviet partisan fighters laying explosives on a railway line behind the German front during the Battle of Kursk, July 1943.

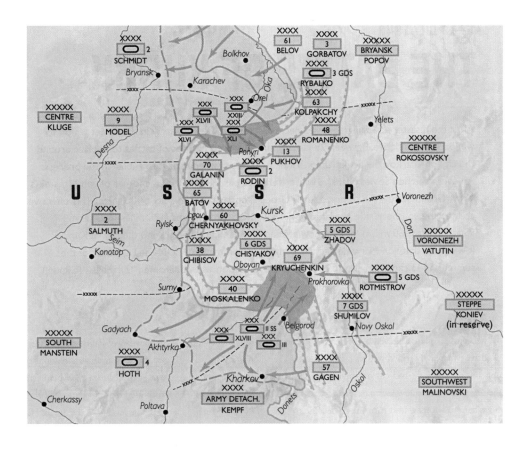

RIGHT Kursk, July–August 1943

German gains after Operation "Zitadelle", 5–13 July

front line, 1 August

front line, 23 August

front line, 23 August

and won support from Stalin, who had wanted an immediate offensive, to build up a heavy defensive shield around Kursk prior to delivering a knock-out blow to the German attackers with large forces held in reserve. The Kursk salient was held by two army fronts, the central front under General Rokossovsky and the Voronezh front under General Vatutin, both of whom had led the defence of Stalingrad. They prepared six separate lines of defence and a complex wall of artillery and anti-tank fire was established. Into the defensive line were moved 1.3 million men, 3,444

29 JUNE 1943
Start of Operation "Cartwheel" designed to roll up Japanese resistance in New Guinea and the islands of the South Pacific.

5–6 JULY 1943
Battle of Kula Gulf off New Heorgia in the Solomons fails to prevent Japanese reinforcement.

10 JULY 1943
Operation "Husky", the Anglo-American invasion of Sicily, begins.

13 JULY 1943
Hitler orders redeployment of German forces to Italy to stem the Allied advance in the Mediterranean theatre.

24 JULY 1943
Start of the bombing campaign against Hamburg in Operation "Gomorrah".

25 JULY 1943
Mussolini is overthrown as Italy's dictator and is arrested.

COLONEL GENERAL HERMANN HOTH
(1885–1971)

The son of an army officer, Hoth joined the army in 1903, fought in the First World War in a variety of roles and stayed on in the postwar 100,000-man force. He rose rapidly during the period of the Third Reich. In October 1938, he commanded the 15th Army Corps and in November that year was made a general. He fought in Poland and France and commanded the 3rd Panzer Group in November 1941, which captured Minsk in the opening weeks of the invasion of the Soviet Union.

In June 1942, he took over command of the 4th Panzer army and fought in the Stalingrad campaign, unsuccessfully leading the effort to rescue Paulus in December 1942. His Panzer group fought at Kursk and later failed to prevent the Soviet reconquest of Kiev, for which he was sacked by Hitler. A ruthless officer, he endorsed harsh measures against Jews and partisans and was convicted at Nuremberg in 1948 of war crimes. He served six years of his 15-year sentence.

LEFT German tanks make their way across the steppe during the Battle of Kursk in July 1943. The confrontation was the largest concentration of tank forces yet seen in the war.

OPPOSITE A destroyed Soviet column during the Battle of Kursk. Although a Soviet victory, the losses of the Red Army amounted to 70,000 dead or captured.

tanks and 2,900 aircraft, around 40 per cent of Soviet manpower and 75 per cent of its armoured force. Both sides treated the huge set-piece battle as a test of strength; the loser risked a great deal.

The Soviet side needed to know when the blow would come, and they were supplied with a large amount of accurate intelligence, but because Hitler kept altering the date there could be no certainty. The "Lucy" spy ring in Switzerland gave the approximate date in early July, but the final date and hour – dawn on 5 July – were found out from kidnapped German

GENERAL NIKOLAI VATUTIN
(1901–44)

Nikolai Vatutin was one of the most successful Soviet generals of the Second World War, though he was only 39 when the USSR was attacked. He served in the Red Army in 1920–21, and then went through formal officer training and a period at the national Frunze Military Academy in 1926, where he proved to be a remarkably talented student and a natural leader. During the purges, he was one of the younger officers rapidly promoted to replace those who had been removed. He became chief-of-staff of the Kiev Special Military District, where he was responsible for organizing the Soviet invasion of eastern Poland in 1939, and in 1940 was promoted to deputy chief of the General Staff where he played a major part in prewar mobilization planning. When war broke out he was sent to Leningrad to stabilize the front and protect the city, and was involved in the defence of Moscow. He commanded the Voronezh Army Group in July 1942, and then the Southwestern Army Group which helped to carry out Operation "Uranus", followed by command of the Voronezh Army Group again for Kursk. He was shot by Ukrainian nationalist partisans on 29 February 1944 and later died of his wounds.

soldiers. The Red Army fired a number of pre-emptive artillery barrages during the night, but the attack went ahead as planned. In the south, General Hoth's 4th Panzer Army, with nine Panzer divisions, crashed forward against the weaker of the two Soviet fronts and in two days it was 30 kilometres (20 miles) towards Kursk, fighting against frantic and stiff opposition. In the north, General Walter Model's 9th Panzer Army was held almost at once by a withering wall of fire. On 6 July, 1,000 tanks were pushed forward on a front only 10 kilometres (six miles) wide towards the town of Ponyri, but by the following day the offensive was bogged down and by 9 July the German northern thrust was halted.

In the south, Hoth's Panzer army moved towards the small town of Prokhorovka where it met the 5th Guards Tank Army commanded by General Pavel Rotmistrov, which had travelled for four days to reach the battlefield. What followed on 12–13 July has usually been described as the largest tank battle of the war, but recent research has suggested that most of the casualties to the Soviet side were caused by Rotmistrov's failure to recognize a Soviet tank trap into which his unfortunate armour blundered. German losses were modest, but the failure in the north and news of the Allied landings in Sicily had led Hitler to cancel the operation on 13 July. Hoth retreated back to where he had started. German commanders failed to realize what would follow because they underestimated Soviet reserves. In the north on 12 July, a massive counter-offensive was launched which liberated Orel on 5 August and Bryansk on 18 August. In the south, the attack was launched on 3 August and by 28 August Kharkov was again in Soviet hands. The way was now open for a general summer offensive to drive back the whole German front.

TRANSLATIONS

PAGE 18: ORDER NO.1 – HITLER'S ORDER TO INVADE POLAND

(Issued by the Supreme Commander of the German armed forces, Berlin, 31.8.39)

Directive No. 1
for the conduct of the war

1.) As all political possibilities to peacefully resolve an intolerable situation on Germany's eastern border have been exhausted, I have decided on a forceful solution.

2.) The attack on Poland must be conducted in accordance with the preparations made for Operation "White" with the modifications resulting from the concentration of troops now almost complete.

Division of tasks and operational objective remain unchanged.

Date of attack: 1.9.39

Time of attack: …..

This time also applies to operations on Gdingen – Danzig Bay and Dirschau Bridge.

3.) With regard to the west, responsibility for opening hostilities must be clearly placed with England and France. Minor frontier violations are, for the time being, only to be confronted on a purely local basis.

The assured neutral status of Holland, Belgium, Luxembourg and Switzerland is to be scrupulously respected.

[Page 2] The German western frontier must not be crossed anywhere on land without my express permission.

On the sea, the same applies to all hostile acts or acts to be interpreted as such.

The defensive measures of the German air force must, for the time being, be absolutely restricted to defence against hostile air attacks on the borders of the Reich during which the frontier with the neutral states is to be respected for as long as possible in repelling individual aircraft and small units. Only when, with the deployment of more intensive French and English aggressive units over the neutral states towards German territory, air defence in the west is no longer secured, are defensive manoeuvres over this neutral territory to be authorized too.

It is particularly important that the supreme command is informed as quickly as possible concerning any infringement of neutrality of third party states by our western opponents.

4.) Should England and France initiate hostilities towards Germany, it is the task of the parts of the German armed forces operating in the west to preserve conditions favourable to a victorious conclusion of the operations against Poland, while protecting our forces as far as possible. In the context of this order, as much damage as possible should be inflicted on hostile forces and the sources of reinforcement of their defence industry. I reserve the right to order the commencement of aggressive action at all times.

[Page 3] The army is holding the West Wall and is making preparations to prevent a pincer movement on it to the north – in the event of a violation of Belgian or Dutch territory by the western powers. Should French forces enter Luxembourg, the blowing up of the border bridges is authorized.

The German navy is waging a trade war with the emphasis being largely against England. To intensify its effectiveness, a declaration of danger zones can be expected. German naval high command (OKM) is to report in which sea territories and the extent to which danger zones are considered appropriate. The text of any public declaration must be prepared in collaboration with the exterior office and submitted to me via supreme command (OKW) for approval.

The Baltic must be secured against enemy incursion. The decision whether to block the entrances to the Baltic with mines will be taken by the German naval high command.

The prime aim of the German air force is to prevent the deployment of the French and English air forces against the German army and German territory.

In the conduct of operations against England, preparations should be made for the deployment of the German air force to disrupt English supplies by sea, the arms industry and troop transports to France. Opportunities favouring an effective attack against massed English fleet units, in particular against battleships and aircraft carriers, must be exploited. Attacks on London are to await my decision.

[Page 4] Preparations must be made for attack on English territory, bearing in mind that inadequate success with incomplete forces must be avoided in all circumstances.

Copies to:

OKH (supreme command of the army) 1st copy

OKM (supreme command of the navy) 2nd copy

R.d.L.u.Ob.d.L. (Reich minister for air travel and supreme commander of the air force) 3rd copy

OKW (supreme command of the armed forces):

Chief WFA (military operations command) 4th copy

L. 5th–8th copies

PAGES 80–81: THE WANNSEE CONFERENCE

[Extracts reproduced here with permission House of Wannsee Conference]
II. SS Lieutenant General [Obergruppenfürher] Heydrich, Head of Security Police and the SD, who opened the meeting with the announcement that the Reich Marshal [Göring] had put him in charge of preparations for the final solution of the Jewish question.

The authority for directing the final solution of the Jewish question rests with the Reichsführer SS and Chief of German Police [ie. Himmler] and Head of the Security Police and the SD [ie. Heydrich], without regard to geographic boundaries.

The Head of the Security Police and the SD [Heydrich] then gave a brief review of the struggle conducted so far against this foe. The most important elements are:

a) forcing the Jews out of the various spheres of the life of the German people,

b) forcing the Jews out of the German people's living space [Lebensraum].

In pursuance of these endeavours, an accelerated emigration of the Jews from the territory of the Reich was seen as the only temporary solution and was accordingly embarked upon in an intensified and systematic manner.

On instruction of the Reich Marshal [ie. Göring], a Reich Central Office for Jewish Emigration was established in January 1939; its direction was entrusted to the Head of the Security Police and the Security Service [SD] [ie. Heydrich]. Its particular tasks were:

a) to take measures for the preparation of increased Jewish emigration,

b) to direct the flow of emigration,

c) to speed up the emigration process in individual cases.

The aim of this task was to purge German living space of Jews by legal means.

III. As a further possible solution, and with the appropriate prior authorization of the Führer, emigration has now been replaced by evacuation to the East. This operation should be regarded only as a provisional option, though in the view of the coming final solution of the Jewish question it is already supplying practical experience of vital importance.

In connection with this final solution of the Jewish question, roughly eleven million Jews will have to be taken into consideration. They are distributed over the individual countries as follows:

In the course of the final solution and under appropriate direction, the Jews are to be utilized for work in the East in a suitable manner. In large labour columns and separately by sexes, Jews capable of working will be dispatched to these regions to build roads, and in the process a large number of them will undoubtedly drop out by way of natural attrition.

Those who ultimately should possibly get by will have to be given suitable treatment because they unquestionably represent the most resistant segments and therefore constitute a natural elite that, if allowed to go free, would turn into a germ cell of renewed Jewish revival. (Witness the experience of history.)

In the course of the practical implementation of the final solution, Europe will be combed through from West to East. Priority will have to be given to the area of the Reich, including the Protectorate of Bohemia and Moravia, if only because of housing shortages and other socio-political needs. The evacuated Jews will first be taken, group after group, to so-called transit ghettos from where they will be transported further East... The intention is not to evacuate Jews over the age of 65 but to send them to an old people's ghetto. Therienstadt has been earmarked for this purpose.

In addition to these age groups – and of the 280,000 Jews who lived in the Altreich and the Ostmark on October 1, 1941, some 30 percent are over 65 – the old people's ghetto will also receive Jews with war injuries and Jews with war decorations (EK I) [Iron Cross First Class]. With this convenient solution the many intercessions [for exemptions from deportation to the East] will be eliminated at one blow.

The onset of the individual major evacuation moves will largely depend on military developments. In regard to the manner in which the final solution will be carried out in those European territories which we now either occupy or influence it has been suggested that the pertinent specialists in the Foreign Office should confer with the appropriate official of the Security Police and the SD [Security Office].

IV. During the implementation plan for the final solution its basis as it were should be the Nuremberg Laws, whereby the solution of the problem of mixed marriages [Mischehen] and mixed parentage [Mischlingen] must likewise be a prerequisite for the definitive settlement of the question.

In conclusion there was discussion about the various types of possible solutions. Herr Gauleiter Dr. Meyer and State Secretary Dr. Bühler both took the position that in connection with the final solution certain preparatory measures be carried out in the occupied territories at once, but in such a way that the population there would be become apprehensive.

The Head of the Security Police and SD [Heydrich] terminated the conference with the request that all participants in today's deliberations give him their co-operation in implementing the tasks connected with the solution.

PAGE 147: PROCLAMATION ISSUED BY HITLER TO GERMAN TROOPS AT STALINGRAD, 26 NOVEMBER 1942

Soldiers of the Sixth Army and the Fourth Panzer Army!

The battle for Stalingrad is reaching its peak.

The enemy has broken through in the rear of the German troops and is now vainly attempting to bring this important stronghold on the Volga back into his possession.

My thoughts and the thoughts of the entire German nation are with you in these hours of hardship.

You must at all costs hold on to the position of Stalingrad, which was won with so much bloodshed under the leadership of your energetic generals!

You must be unswerving in your resolve, as in Kharkov in spring, to ensure that the Russians will be annihilated by this breakthrough.

I shall do everything in my power to support you in your heroic struggles.

Adolf Hitler

INDEX

CREDITS

I am happy to acknowledge the extent to which this book has been a real team effort. The book's editor Gemma Maclagan has played a key part in getting the book together and keeping me on schedule.

Russell Knowles and Steve Behan are responsible for the book's strong visual content and layout.

Philip Parker and Terry Charman have between them made sure that the history is as error-free as it can be and I am grateful to them for their scrupulous monitoring of the text and captions which has made this a better book.

The majority of photographs reproduced in this book have been taken from the collections of the Photograph Archive at the Imperial War Museum. The reference numbers for each of the photographs are listed below, giving the page number, location and reference number.

Key: t = top, b = bottom, c = centre, l = left & r = right

9 Department of Documents, 12 t CH 1297, 15 HU 5358, 18-19 Department of Documents, 22 D 2597, 28 NYP 68075, 29 l F4849, 29 r HU 1135, 30 t COL 294, 30 c O 177, 30-31 H 1647, 34 HU 3266, 35 HU 2283, 37 83/15/11 Department of Documents, 39 CH 1398, 40 HU 4481, 41 t CH 1401, 41 b CM 3513, 42 H 3096, 43 H 667, 44-45 H 3640, 45 A 10296, 46-47 Department of Documents, 50-51 HU 1129, 53 HU 39455, 54 tl INS 804, 57 b A 4386, 64 E 3464, 67 E 4087, 68 EN 21474, 74 t NYP 45042, 74 b NY 7343, 75 courtesy Brigadier J Percival, 83 H 17365, 90 SE 3310, 94 t TR 11, 94 b CH 13020, 96 l C 2615, 108-113 couresty Major H D Lyttleton, 120 A 11231, 121 TR 2625, 123 t C 3193, 123 c 3193, 123 b 3193, 128 E 18980, 130-131 Department of Documents, 133 A 12649, 147 (816 XX02 Spec Misc B6)

Photographs from sources from outside the Imperial War Museum:

AKG Images: 33 t, 54-55, 62l, 63, 76, 122-123, 124, 145t, 146, 151b, 152, 154

Churchill Archives Centre, Churchill College, Cambridge: 59

Curtis Brown Ltd, London on behalf of The Estate of Winston Churchill: 36

De Agostini Picture Library 5, 125

Getty Images: 144b; /AFP 16 t; /Austrian Archives 10; /Bettmann 24, 70, 93; /Central Press 51; /Corbis 26 b, 27, 62r, 73; /Fox Photos 20, 21;

/Haynes Archive/Popperfoto 127 b; /Hugo Jaeger/Timepix/The LIFE Picture Collection 7 t; /Hulton Archive 49, 52, 151t; /Hulton-Deutsch Collection/CORBIS 12 b, 17, 25; /Keystone 54, 69, 72, 126-127, 140; /Keystone/Hulton Archive 22;/ TIME Magazine/Time & Life Pictures 7 b, 67 r, 77 t, 91, 92; /Topical Press Agency 16 b, 33 b; /Tree Lions 11

House of the Wannsee Conference: 80-81

Library & Archives, Canada: 123 b

The National Archives, Kew: 57 t (DEFE3-2-122), 84-85 (PREM3-32-1-27)

National Archives & Records Administration, Washington: 71, 87, 88-89, 89, 98, 100-105, 114t, 114b, 116, 117t, 118, 134-137, 141-143

PA Images: 97

Photo12: Collection Bernard Crochet 61t; /Hachedé 8

Private Collection: 117b, 118, 139

Photo Scala, Florence/bpk, Bildagentur fuer Kunst, Kultur und Geschichte, Berlin: 155

Shutterstock: AP 26 t, 138, 139

Topfoto: 77 b, 129, 150; /Ullstein Bild 66 l, 79, 96 r, 107l, 107r, 126b, 149, 153

Ullstein Bild: 61b

United States Holocaust Memorial Museum: 78

Every effort has been made to acknowledge correctly and contact the source and/or copyright holder of each picture and Welbeck Publishing apologises for any unintentional errors or omissions, which will be corrected in future editions of this book.